IN COLOR

Resilience from rock bottom

Awareness from adversity

JG GARCIA

*Donations will be given to animal rescue organizations
from the book's proceeds. Mahalo for your kōkua.*

In Color: Resilience from rock bottom
Awareness from adversity

JG Garcia

As You Wish Publishing Phoenix, Arizona

All rights reserved. No part of this book may be reproduced or transmitted in any form or by any means, electronic or mechanical, including photo-copying, recording, or any information storage and retrieval system, without written permission from the author, exceptfor the inclusion of brief quotations in a review.

Copyright © 2021 As You Wish Publishing

ISBN 13 - 978-1-951131-37-1

Library of Congress Control Number - 2021920568

Published in the United States of America

For more information, visit the publisher's website at:
www.asyouwishpublishing.com.

No part of this book is a substitute for mental or physical health. If you need help please seek it.

*My grandmother Avelina Delos Reyes
& my uncle Mario Delos Reyes*

*From conception to completion,
I wrote with you in mind.*

*The truth is like a lion.
You don't have to defend it.
Let it loose. It will defend itself.
- St. Augustine of Hippo*

CONTENTS

AUTHOR'S NOTE i
PREQUEL iii

I – SILVER SCREEN 1
   1. OUTTAKES 3
   2. FACE THE AUDIENCE 9
   3. BEST SUPPORTING ACTOR 19

II – RED FLAGS 29
   4. EYE OF THE STORM 31
   5. TROUBLE IN PARADISE 41

III – BLACKOUT 51
   6. PULL THE PLUG 53
   7. LIGHTS OUT 59

IV – GO GREEN 69
   8. SPRING CLEANING 71
   9. RULES OF DISENGAGEMENT 85
   10. IT'S A RAP 95

V – TICKLE PINK 103
   11. BABY TALK 105
   12. DINNER AND A MOVIE 117
   13. NOW AND MAYBE FOREVER 129

VI – TRUE BLUE 137

    14. TWO + TWO 139

    15. THANK YOU, DON'T COME AGAIN 151

VII – PURPLE HEARTS 161

    16. LAVENDER 163

    17. MAN UP 179

    18. SAY NO TO THE DRESS..................................... 194

VIII – YELLOW BRICK ROAD 205

    19. THE MIDAS TOUCH 207

    20. DO NOT DISTURB.. 213

    21. THANK HEAVEN 219

    22. FUREVER... 231

    23. GOLIATH 235

MAHALO NUI LOA…………..………………....251

AUTHOR'S NOTE

"Stick to the facts." – Joseph Nadzady

One of the best advice I've ever received.

My friend and former supervisor Joe taught me this in 2008 after working together at The Washington Hospital Center in D.C. He's an avuncular leader, a devoted husband and father, a gifted artist, and a man of faith who has not only mentored me in my career with his astuteness, insights, and impeccable work ethics, but also bettered me as a person. In this regard, it's my sincere intent to relay my stories and unbiased views with factual accounts. These events were transcribed from my personal standpoint and through the filter of my own understanding, ergo could differ from the versions of those who shared them with me. With consent, I referenced people by their real names (*the world needs to know these endearing souls*), and for the privacy of others, I changed theirs. Overall, this book's written with densely documented facts and good evidence—verifiable evidence.

More on Joe later.

For now, as we say here on island, *Aloha É Komo Mai…*

PREQUEL

September 5, 2017
Bali, Indonesia

"You've activated parts of my heart, JG, parts I didn't know existed, and I thank you for that... it's hard to explain, but I can feel things inside me, not just around me, like before: joy, sadness, pain, excitement. It's like when someone is color blind—they could only see things in black and white. All their life, everything was black and white—and then, for the first time—they see in color."

-D

September 23, 2017
Honolulu, Hawaii

Double rainbows, pastel skies, and yearly sunshine. How lucky are we to live in Hawaii? It's been our playground since 2013, and to say it's idyllic can't delineate the half of it. My husband Carlos and I swapped our Cleveland Park condo in the upland landscape of D.C. for a two bedroom high-rise apartment on the Ala Wai, the unobstructed views of Connecticut Avenue for vignettes of the Pacific, and politics for pineapple. We used to regale in haute couture and Christian Dior, with champagne, upscale hors d'oeuvres, pan-ethnic cuisines, Martinis, and Merlot ,over Democratic demagogueries and Republican repartee, but now—in flip flops and T-shirts—we're living the life!

What's more splendid than the shorelines of Haleʻiwa and the gusting breeze of the Koʻolau is our cheerful, motley crew of friends, *"The Troops."* Like the sitcom *Friends,* our crib, *"Casa de Martinez,"* is ground zero *Central Perk.* And they're also constants in our home! It's so kosher with these chums, from skydiving to snide banters, spontaneous karaoke to holiday festivities, sugar sprinkled malasadas to apricot facials, brisket to bento, *anything* goes.

And other obstreperous, Rated X shenanigans…

Why this gang, particularly Carlos' workout wingman and best friend Paul—an eligible F-22 pilot physician, who's been ready for *"the one"* since he was nineteen, a man who could grace the cover of *G.Q.* with his washboard abs, and have his pick—prefers to be with us than to be out in town?

"He wants what we have, babe," Carlos boasted.

The tropical vibe of a laid-back lifestyle is a health benefit to me and my jittery Type A personality and a placating compliment to my husband's California cool disposition. With O'ahu's proximity to the Philippines and L.A., we're in the same hemisphere with our *ohanas (families)*. Carlos stays active by hiking and snorkeling; I get my Zen on with eco-minded yogis. We have no kids, no fish, no plants—just our vim and vigor pampered by picturesque sunsets, pristine beaches, and gorgeous climate. A quilt of cultures interwoven from Polynesia makes our dishes universally robust to cater to globe-trotting palettes and locals alike. We devour *poké* by day, star-gaze with Mai Tai by night—hammock optional. *Pero* there's a famine of memorable Mexican eateries on the island. *No es mi problema*! I'm married to a Mexican who makes ceviche like no other. From the Waikiki skyline to the Windward terrains, in this melting pot, we live, breathe, and emanate the spirit of aloha. We have the best of both worlds.

Today is just another day in paradise. We cuddled and did what lovers do on an idle Saturday morning. Island time is slow time, so I stayed supine on rumpled sheets, and Carlos kissed me goodbye before watching the driving lesson of one of *"The Troops."* I'll meet the gals later for *pupus* and *lilikoi*. By midday, *kama'āina* artisans and Spam vendors were afoot for a street festival, and ukuleles and reggae serenaded the tourists as a kaleidoscope of demographic groups thronged across Kālakaua Avenue. By dinnertime, Carlos was home. I invited him to join us for dessert.

As foretold, he walked a short distance from our apartment to The Moana Surfrider. Tides were lapping. I finished my first lemonade with a second one coming when he arrived.

"Where is everybody?" He was bemused.

"No, it's just us."

He asked if everything's ok. I signaled him to sit, I turned over the documents on the table, pushed the pages under his hands, and locked his eyes with mine. Then whiplash.

"Carlos, I'm letting you go."

His hands quavered. Divorce papers.

"Are you serious?"

He looked pasty and panicked, his tone, tremulous.

Am I serious?

I've been imagining this moment since October of 2011, and there's *nothing* unplanned about its machination.

I flew my Mum in yesterday from Maryland after a three-day notice. She was just partying in Vegas and hadn't quite unpacked from that trip. She's four feet away from Carlos, hiding and squinting behind bushes twice her height. Last night, I left a satchel of clothes and documents in her hotel.

Girlfriend #1 is plopping behind the same thickets with her camera peering right at us. Her chair was next to Mum's. Girlfriend #2 is lounging without much stealth by the pool across from us—also with her camera. Carlos never met her. She's unfamiliar and has the best seat in the house.

These women were pent up with anxiety, but in the event of an impetuous pushback, they were prepared to intervene.

Last month, I flew to Baguio City and opened up to my sis Marian (*volleyball queen*). She's now in church, lightning every candle in Baguio, waiting for my call.

My pal Dylan, a lawyer whose legal tutelage I solicited had been prepping me for months without any billable hours.

My official attorney, the male Laura Wasser of family law, battened down the decree without ever calling my cell or sending an invoice to my email or home mailbox. He knew my situation was exigent, *anyone* could be suspect, and that time was of the essence, so even our meetings were laconic. Up to this point, he didn't exist.

For the second time in my life, all concerted efforts were focused on fleeing. Isolation and fear ran deep in this covert orchestration—a surreptitious exit plagiarized out of Katie Holmes' playbook. Contrary to others' presumptions, I didn't move to Hawaii for its perks, but to complete a mission that was arduous, if not impossible, when executed in traditional terms. It took me five years, eleven months, three days, and seven people to pull it off. I couldn't have choreographed these surefire strategies if they weren't in cahoots with me.

As for yours truly? Earlier this September, I formulated the homestretch of this bombshell on international soil—Bali soil. A sideshow and a geographical gambit that gave me a toehold to plot away from premonitions and prying eyes. Upon returning, I got a new cellphone, with a new number, under my own name. I saw people Carlos and I knew when I careened to my lawyer's downtown office, but I let my frizzy, raven-black hair undulate past my hip—an image that stood in stark polarity to my customary ash-blonde ponytail. I was unrecognizable.

As for the catalyst, *not* the cause, of this decision? There's someone else….

He's a pious believer, a renaissance man—a good friend and a better person, whose frankness outrivals my own. An undercurrent of illicit—but guarded—attraction had been brewing in more ways I'd like to admit, before we deplaned in Bali—a subconscious yearning reined back by platonic undertones. During those watershed evenings in Seminyak, denude of my veneer, I unburdened to him the bleak secrets of my moribund marriage. He felt like home as we blurred the line in sweet surrender—beyond a point we shouldn't have gone. Between right and wrong, my world came to a surreal standstill. Uncharacteristically unguarded, I drifted away, falling into him—deeper than sin. Nothing done that wasn't consented; nothing felt that wasn't implied. In those fleeting moments, I was alive; I'd lived, but not before him. All in the passage of those untimely nights spent through an hourglass, we were *"one person, two bodies."* My mirror. My silver lining. My missing piece. Joy so unadulterated, it's ineffable; happiness so unbridled, it's forbidden. Never had I coveted anyone like this—from my sinew to my soul. My heart, no regrets. Others saw me one way; he another. I'd give my all to relive it; let my hair down again—as he liked. On the off chance there's a forever, he'd be the only one. But even then, eternity would not be endless enough. Airborne back to O'ahu, we agreed to keep a safe distance; not overstep our bounds until I was unfettered—heart freed, hands untied. I called his name in silent adoration because detaching from him felt like telling myself not to breathe. How I needed him, more than I'd ever needed, more than I was allowed to need... Emblazoned in my flesh is his face.

And his words: *"When the dust settles, I'll be waiting."*

But what is all an illusion? Far worse, a lie?

I leaned into Carlos and said, *"You may have stalled me, but you didn't stop me."*

Carlos knew what I meant; he could read that chyron. His deafening silence ratified my words landed in the right spot, and in that instant, his world abruptly stopped. He was blindsided, but he knew I've had enough with the dilatory theatrics—and had been for some time. He knew there was nothing left to contemplate or contest. He knew this was our season's shocking finale. No trilogy.

My husband had gone to unusual lengths to keep me; I had to resort to drastic depths to leave him. I couldn't have escaped swiftly—not after my first attempt went haywire. When you're left with one *last* chance for freedom, you revise your plan deftly and with surgical precision. All was timed with maximum restraint and prophylactic measures.

I've longed for this day as much as I've feared it for the only thing worse than the disgrace of a divorce is the sham of this marriage and the illusory life I've resigned myself to live. It is a fate worse than death.

On the outward is this mirage of marital and personal bliss, but backstage, even now as the cracks crumble, the reality is you couldn't absorb the unmentionable depravities I've buried under the auspice of artificial happiness—even if you try. But today's a new day.

I'm ready.

Now.

Finally.

Joy awaits.

Waves swooshed as Mum and I moseyed on down Kūhiō Avenue—past the partygoers—to her hotel on Kānekapōlei Street. I smiled as their roistering followed us—joining in their revelry. It was a sigh of relief. At last, a clean slate. I can start afresh and rebuild. The rest will take care of itself. I've been set free. This nightmare's over.

Or has it just begun?

I – SILVER SCREEN

"To be yourself in a world that is constantly trying to make you something else is the greatest accomplishment."
- Ralph Waldo Emerson

1. OUTTAKES

"I became insane, with long intervals of horrible sanity."
- Edgar Allan Poe

Anachronisms are onscreen misfits—people, places, and things that are chronologically out of place, but they help satirize stories, establish connections between eras, and incorporate humor and mystique with a diegesis twist. In *Back to the Future*, "*Johnny B. Goode*" was sung during a 1955 prom—the song didn't come out until 1958. Filmmakers, screenwriters, and playwrights use anachronisms intentionally or unintentionally to appeal to their audience and make the plot relatable and believable. Sometimes, the shimmer of synchrony and special effects is so believable, theatergoers don't see the inaccuracies even when they're superimposed with the truth. The turnout sees only the matinee—and it's marvelous.

You can see anachronisms in preeminent works such *Marie Antoinette, Braveheart,* and *Napoleon Dynamite*, and as far back as *Hamlet* and *Macbeth*. But for others, they don't need to look much further to find things that are not at all what they seem. I wouldn't know…

Once a hayseed from the Philippines and daddy's Disney princess, I'm now at the stratosphere of life, married to my best friend, the hallmark of success, a super-woman gussied up for cotillions, and lithe in an agglomeration of expensive shoes and velveteen ballgowns. Hefty paychecks. Résumé of renowned names. Condo. Penthouse. Fancy zip codes. Corporate ladder. Everything's just dandy!

And cut…

In 1990, my family nicknamed me "*Butterfly*" before I left the Philippines to live with my parents abroad. So naïve, so innocent. Since then, they think I've been floating through an impressive and inspiring life, sipping margaritas, but the lights in the photographs weren't as incandescent as they seemed—the shellac, not so smooth. I've lived my years in total variance with the patina of perfection. I've felt things, done things, seen things, and heard things no child should witness—under the most abominable conditions little ones should not endure.

Not one childhood immunization inoculated me from the godawful world where under the rubric of strength, I was *always* in character—a clampdown on emotional nudity was the caveat of my survival. Because I was entrapped in battles before I learned how to fight, I'm no stranger to darkness, and I know evilness by name. I've played the part of the earnest pupil, the blushing bride, and the obedient daughter, all with aplomb—dutiful in my stead, to the lies I've created, and to those I've tried to please.

Never flouting. Never flipping the script. Half-human and half-robot; it played to my strength.

Concealing my weakness *is* my strength. It is a gift and a curse of comparable harm.

But behind the scenes was a washout woman, an estranged daughter, a wretched wife, and not much else—down to her last remnant of hope. A brilliant actress fooling the world, but mostly fooling herself.

At age ten, I was dreaming among the stars. At forty, I was sifting myself from the ashes. Porous with nonexistent parameters and a step away from the fall, divorce pushed me over the edge. A balancing act, then a burnout, and finally, a breaking point. At the core of my character, I was diffident and frail. Past defending. Past pretending. Despite having a high threshold for pain, I realized even the grittiest of us have an Achilles' heel.

The anguish was beyond anything I've ever experienced; the rumors beyond fallacious. But it didn't stop bystanders from jabbering judgments, threats, perennial lies, and more rumors, by mouth, in writing, and on the airwaves—like a coordinated ambush. Looking back, I could've saved these critics the hassle by telling them the most boisterous note of negativity, beratement, and voice of vitriol were the ones playing in my head.

But it was the betrayals that bruised down to the bones.

Trusted friends are to be ever present in times of trouble. Where are they now? Now that my life's awry, and I need my platoon to pull me through. House empty. Troops gone. Were they just seasonal sidekicks?

My health took a nosedive. My faith was at its all-time low. Fear did a number on me, and I hit the ground terrified into retreat as an utter collapse unlocked the floodgates of hell that I called home. With historical wounds wide open, my rueful choices caught up with me with lessons I was neither willing nor ready to learn—not in this desolation I could no longer downplay. Depleted, I would've traded the truth for a vestige of love or scrap of security—anything but a deep dive into my double life.

I knelt in humble worship and asked God if He was angry at me for abjuring His teachings and seceding from my church. I didn't know if I should cling tighter to a crucifix talisman I no longer believed in, and asked for forgiveness from a God I couldn't see, for leaving a man I didn't love, or to just take a knee in silent supplication.

There was my wedding dress tucked away in the closet—compressed with a crimped edge, single-tier veil. And there I was—triple A: alone; awake; aware. Alone in a purgatory of my own making and with the memories therein. Awake from the outside looking in on autopilot. Aware of the sting of shame and stigma from the solemn vows I've broken. With my arms draped in satin, my fingers quivered along the mermaid silhouette as tears streamed down my face and drizzled on the cathedral train.

What's happening to me?

I was an expert at this! I used to ad-lib under the guise of anything and everything, but now—unscripted—I'm not even a whit of what I used to be. In this reality, every night felt longer than the last. The pain was unrelenting. Is this as unrelenting as it gets? And if this were a foretaste of life without my husband, then there's not much left of it to live.

There's not much left of me.

Where do I go from here? Where do I go from him?

Still hunching over my dress—the last token of my safe prison—I wailed in agony and pressed the laced corset over my mouth to insulate the howling. My skin was clammy, my breath, raspy. I felt my innards curdling as I gasped for air, but couldn't muster a shed of strength to ascend to the surface. I slouched against the wall and bellowed into a fetal position. I broke in half then asunder.

I feel asleep as I fell apart.

I've acted out this drama for twenty-seven years—it didn't look like I'd survive it in less than one.

I woke up swathed in wrinkled fabrics as a pillow and the closet floor, my bed. Languor above, tulle below.

This divorce was the death blow. Not saying prior punches were less lethal, but this was purely the irrevocable crack in my already mashed safety shell.

> *"If you can't fly, then run, if you can't run, then walk, if you can't walk, then crawl, but whatever you do, you have to keep moving forward."*
> - Dr. Martin Luther King, Jr.

I crawled onto my mattress and watched the bedroom walls cave in. I wept my eyes shut into another daybreak.

Tomorrow, maybe I could try to walk.

2. FACE THE AUDIENCE

"No man, for any considerable period can wear one face to himself and another to the multitude, without finally getting bewildered as to which may be true."
- Nathaniel Hawthorne

Valedictory speeches are condensed keynotes of life lessons, indelible memories, and notable academic achievements. The intro sets the oration's tone, the body recites lachrymose anecdotes imbued with clichés and bumper stickers, and the windup offers an ode of gratitude to spectators and parents and imparts wisdom to the grads. Valedictorians who outrank their peers across all measures of merit are still among a pantheon of dignitaries, so on the rostrum, they comply with a formulaic sequence of public speaking and deliver their lines per protocol—like I did.

Not today. Today, I intend to make some noise.

"When people appear to be excelling externally, they may still be suffering internally. By sharing your own struggles, you make it easier for others to open up about theirs."
- Psychologist Dr. Adam Grant, Ph.D.

I strived for above average in the classroom, but in life, I settled for mediocrity.

Over the substrates, I catapulted to majestic heights, but the indescribable traumas, regrets, and consequences I reaped occurred below deck. My world was sculpted by pyrrhic victories. For thirty some years, I wrangled with issues that social mores instructed me never to say out loud. Ensnared in sorrow, but chary of looking like a wuss, I hid and waited for someone to normalize what I felt, but was too ashamed to expose—like so many others. I waited for them to share their stories, not realizing the power of my own.

In the wake of divorce, I gained knowledge and awareness so profound, it'd be a disservice to those ready to dig their own graves if I were to keep them to myself. I realized grief knows neither faction nor race, and hardships don't hand out dispensation to any organized religion or gender orientation. Our stories are less about losses and failures than they are about interlaced experiences that cleave us together in our resolve. I learned in our struggles, we want to know we are not alone.

Stories aren't made by our formidable exteriors, but by our pathologies. Haven't we all been in rough waters? Hate, betrayal, abuse, death, domestic violence, unsteady careers, mental illness, disabilities, eating disorders, marital deceits, family secrets, financial strife, checkered pasts, loneliness, maladaptive lifestyles, dizzying relationships, rape, anger, isolation, suicide… In many ways, our stories are woven with the common thread of tragedy. It fluctuates in weight, not in kind. These toxins are around us; we just call them by different names.

Do we not sweep these nuisances under the carpet and into the grubby habitat in which they thrive? We trivialize the truth, whitewash drawbacks, and dilute disillusionments.

When stories are sanitized, real becomes rare.

In my writings, by pulling back the curtains on these taboo topics, I reached out—and from the cramped enclosures of their hearts, others had reached back—judgement reserved. Our worlds differed, but our need for compassion was the same. In showing my scars, I felt human; in a community,

I felt hope. When we see collective grief, collegial courage, and shared vulnerability as tapestries of our social bonds, we realize life isn't so solitary after all.

In this book, I wrote about these thorny issues—not with humiliation—but with gratitude for having survived them.

Untethered. Unmasked. Unfiltered. Uncut.

Unlike stodgy speeches—a spiel from beginning to end—maybe this book could develop dialogues, and I welcome contrarian stances. What it won't do is browbeat you into disaffirming your philosophies or adopting mine without debate—enough of that's going around. It's not a one-size-fits-all solution, a panacea for all ailments of humankind, or a one-stop-shop school of thought that will blaze the trail and turn your life around over-night. I'm still learning the ropes! I'm neither above nor ahead of you, but beside you on this capricious zig-zag called "*Life.*" There's no manual for its unknown or database for its mysteries.

I pray through examples from my own life that you'll see yourself in my story, and honor your own.

I have an antipathy to small talks (*my kryptonite*), so some pages are devoid of circumlocutory preambles. Banal chats lack bluntness, and bluntness and breviloquent save time. If you want your coffee with cream, I'm not your gal. I prefer poignant and provocative talks that refute misconceptions, disabuse me of my thinking errors, enliven the mind, and arouse the soul. Like an umpire, I call balls and strikes.

How else could you have progress and change?

In his 2003 Harvard commencement soliloquy, actor Will Ferrell said, *"I've decided to do one thing that a lot of people are probably afraid to do, and that is to give it to you straight... I graduated from the University of Life. I received a degree from the School of Hard Knocks... And I'm sorry, but I refuse to sugarcoat it."*

Find his words resonant?

A rollcall: all you train wrecks with deferred dreams, unmet priorities and unsound minds; spiritually sapped; physically enfeebled; mentally exhausted; loved by a few; betrayed by a batch; underrated; disheartened; in a crux of a catastrophe or at the end of your rope; squeamish about the future; in a quagmire of the past; unsure of the now, amorphous with boundaries; dissuaded by barriers; taming demons day in, day out; self-doubting; self-sacrificing; dissipating time; splurging money; hankering for support; burning bridges, lingering at rock bottom; and/or sliding over the brink of a breakdown—let's talk. You're in good company.

If you have it all figured out, this book is *not* for you.

This is for those who believe they're good people who'd taken a few wrong turns and are trying to stay in motion as much as the next person while doing their best with the hand they've been dealt with. Some of you may have more mileage on this expedition while others are still untangling themselves from things that serve no constructive purpose. However far you've skewed off course, whatever deterrents life had launched at you or morbid conditions you've been under, whatever lessons you've learned or wish to unlearn, and wherever you are on the road to recovery—you're still here—not cowering but showing up even in the midst of the most unfavorable odds. I applaud your resilience.

And I know there's a story there.

> *"There's no greater agony than bearing an untold story inside you."* - Poet and guru Maya Angelou

Your story is seething within—own it—it's highs and lows. You have a voice, and it is of value. Your heart is a sizable depository of acumen and blessings waiting to be distilled. If you can inspire others to hold on for another minute, stand another hour, or live another day, transform yourself from a victim to a victor, and let the words seep out. Be an agent of change, and transmute your mess into a message.

This is how connections are fortified, how crucial we are to each other, and how we get to be in communion when we fall, just as we celebrate when we rise. Servanthood isn't about curated inventories of *"Comments"* and *"Likes"*; it's about connections and their impact. If exuded with candor and honesty, your story will strike a chord with someone, at some juncture, at some level. (*Appropriate*) self-disclosure and transparency can set the stage for others to follow suit.

I know laying your heart disrobed poses a salvo of backlash and unpleasant ramifications. I tried verbal restraint with details of my divorce, and I still got tarred by erroneous lies diffused by those without a shred of interest in the truth. Whether I was the angel or the demon in those groundless narrations depended on which parodies they heard or were hoodwinked to hear. I bet they didn't hear the unabridged story that didn't leave out pertinent facts.

"Your ex-wife sounds like a really awesome person!" said no one ever.

Here's my point: you could be the hero in your story and be the villain in someone else's—people *will* judge you and do so viciously. Posse of trolls and social media subordinates will insult you and do so ruthlessly. Your stories need not be The Gettysburg Address or The Sermon on the Mount. If you have the truth on your side, face the assembly.

Here comes the noise.

Unfortunately, we now live in an insular ecosystem where everyone finds *everything* offensive—from leprechauns to mascots. Even innuendoes cannot be innuendos! Comedian Bill Maher calls these crybabies *"emotional hemophiliacs, the least little thing will make them start to bleed."* If you step on their toes or hit a primal nerve, it'll be open season for obloquy, ignominy, and unbidden ratings and reviews.

Make a politically wrong sound and media marionettes will dox you for a misnomer or a hyperbole you said five, ten, fifteen years ago, misreport and mischaracterize you, take the worst interpretation of everything you say, caricature your faith and family, and drag your reputation through the gutter—and theirs. If you go against the grain of medieval manifestos, you may be scourged, prohibited from getting a job, your business subsidized, sales embargoed, book deal revoked, even your license disbarred. When you're making enemies left and right, who'll believe you? You'd wish to put that genie back in the bottle.

When the German Chancellor called the wholesale speech boycotting in America *"problematic,"* you know you're in trouble (*what does she know? Did something happen there in the 1930s?*).

And in today's political status, you'll be scapegoated by scoundrels with no sliver of self-awareness for upheavals they engender themselves. And this voice-crippling cartel is coming to a district near you.

> *"We realize the importance of our voice when we are silenced."* - Nobel Prize laureate Malala Yousafzai

From criticism to censorship, if tech oligarchs think your message's heresy, it's cancellation galore! You can't speak! Nicolás Maduro, Ayatollah Khamenei, Antifa, Bill Ayers, Louis Farrakhan, and genocidal Chinese communists can, but you can't!

If they can't shut you up with nonsensical thoughts, they'll just pull labels out of their colons: you racist; sexist; fascist; misogynist; jihadist; supremacist; terrorist; insurrectionist; conspiracist—*stay with me*—Xenophobic; Islamophobic; homophobic; transphobic; oppressor; agitator; colonizer; Klansman; sectarian; totalitarian—*almost there*—infidel; mansplaining maggot; Uncle Tom; Uncle Tim; Neo-Nazi; despot; Coon; bible thumping; gun and religion clinging; blacklisted human manure; cult of ugly chumps; ISIS-ish; Al-Qaeda-ish; Taliban-ish; basket of deplorables who must be deplatformed, dehumanized, and deprogrammed.

Feel the unity yet? The empathy?

But if your story—your narrative—is politically appealing, they'll turn the valve down to the lullabies of Barney and Elsa, make a hackneyed call for hand holding and healing, and get you on the *"Kumbaya"* bandwagon—Soviet style.

I'm appalled by the duplicity.

Are you?

And in that spirit, dare I ask, do you have one prototype of guiding principles? They say in this country, we have two systems of justice. Do *you* have two systems of atrocities, two systems of outrage, two systems of compassion?

You're either telling the truth or you're lying; you either proscribe inflammatory rhetoric or you don't; you either excoriate incompetence or you don't; you either want to defund x, y, z or you don't.

No option B, and one degree of deviation is hypocrisy.

>D-o-u-b-l-e. S-t-a-n-d-a-rd. H-y-p-o-c-r-i-s-y.

I told you—left, right, and center—I'll call it as it is.

I don't care if you're among a cavalcade of *Who's Who* or in a forum full of lepers. Do you have the courage to stand for what you believe? The conviction to pick a lane and stay in it? To tell the emperor he has no clothes?

If you'll uplift and unite, not degrade and divide or pep for peace, not parrot a propaganda… if you remember there's a time and a lectern for *everything*: for dribbling; storytelling; eulogizing; and flapping your gums about parity of income, wind turbines, your contraceptives, and filibuster…

If you won't inveigle us into thinking good is evil, disunity is unity, moderate is radical, north is south, east is west, men versus women, black versus white, rich versus poor...

If you won't contravene your own edicts or reprove those who don't affirm them (*rules for thee but not for me*)…

If you won't urinate on my leg, and tell me it's raining…

If you won't be smug with selective morality only when the moment serves you or be sanctimonious only when it's your side, your story, or your safety that's at stake…

If you won't holler for diversity and inclusivity, then bully others into talking and thinking the same or tell people their skin is their sin or their race is a disgrace…

If you'll tell your story as a disciple of the truth—not his truth, her truth, your truth, or my truth (*this was my motto, so I'm guilty of this*), not ideological truth, not subjective truth, not politically correct truth, not media malfeasance truth, not a scintilla of truth—but *the* truth and the whole truth, then go ruffle some feathers. Go rattle that cage.

3. BEST SUPPORTING ACTOR

"Before you heal someone, ask him if he's willing to give up the things that make him sick."
- Hippocrates

I knew I was disinterested in Carlos from the get-go, but after a month of dating, something shook my certainty. We went to the movies in Alexandria, Virginia with my friend Charlene (*the only one who knew we're together*) and her husband Ryan—a double date. Maybe being with a couple inside a theater full of lovers could fan a spark of attraction inside me. Carlos wasn't so voluble that evening, and Charlene gave him a thumbs up for conducting himself so well. Frigid and famished on that December night, we grabbed a quick bite, and midway through dinner, both gentlemen offered to walk to the ticket booth.

They returned empty handed.

"What's wrong, babe? No more seats?" I asked.

"They changed the time. We can wait a few hours to see what you like or we can watch something else now. I want to check with you first before I decide. What do you want to do, *mí amor?*" Carlos asked.

We looked at each other in agreement: let's wait. We could stroll around the pier to pass time. Carlos kissed me before heading out with Ryan to get the cars. Then I boohooed like a faucet of tears and snot.

"What—is—wrong—with—you—JG?"

"Oh my God, Sis! He checked with me first! He loves me! He thought of me! He cares so much! I am his priority!"

Charlene looked at me as if I were hallucinating on LSD.

It was a moment unheard of for me up until that night. In terms of priority from men, it was a doozy and more than I've ever received.

Two weeks later—around Christmas, before New Year's—he moved in. Three weeks after that, he proposed. Carlos was a garrulous, sly, Gen Y, Bruce Willis lookalike full of inappropriate puns, but on the bright side, we both loved Japanese art, samurai flicks, a roundhouse, katana, bokken, and Kanji logographic. He was a jujitsu diehard, I aikido.

I disliked the rest of him, but Carlos *could* change—and I had the magic wand to make it happen.

He wasn't the first man I tried to tinker with, but the most uncultured among the previous contenders who auditioned for my hand in marriage, so I upped the ante—and what a calamitous calculation that was. I floundered on one, and I sure floundered on the next. Why didn't I quit while I was ahead? Because I drank the love Kool-Aid. Because I was Marquis de Sade with a Messianic complex. And because I thought I could plan the lives of these men better than they could plan themselves. There were incidental abrasions, but these front runners were the deepest cuts:

Bronze finalist - the nerdy, effeminate guy from church. Baptized with the sobriquet *"The Filipino Kenny G"* for his knack for the saxophone, this songbird fawned over me on the piano with melodies and arias. I was his protégé, and together, we worked with victims of domestic violence. He cared for the lesser among us; I respected him for that. An austere Catholic, Peter put a premium on abstinence. He wanted to have a family immediately after getting his Ph.D.

His life was preplanned. Peter was comfortable, safe, and a bit too vanilla. I thought I could vamp him with oomph and effervescence, but our engagement had a shorter shelf life than a jar of mustard. He was good to me; he loved me, but he loved his aspirations more. He was who he was, and I met a classmate—a dapper bloke with a zing (*Mr. Silver*). Vanilla bean and I parted ways, and I returned the three-stone, two-carat, pear-cut diamond. A year later, he wrote me stating, "*I never should've let you go.*"

Peter met another Filipina—also a nurse—and married her.

Silver - the Santa Cruz bloke named Jonathan. Exceedingly competitive and flamboyantly ambitious. This college fling started without so much as a week of intermission from Peter, making it all the more steamy and frenetic. Our class didn't think we'd last longer than our pediatric rotation—I know—they betted on it. He was scholastically nimble and ostentatious—he lorded it over me every time. We watched sailboats in Annapolis and had filet mignon and caviar in Baltimore's ritziest restaurants—in lieu of rubbing elbows with the dregs of society—he was much too debonair for that. We were a powerhouse, but we provoked the worst in each other. With his wry nature and my pugnacious mouth, benign disaccords turned foul, torrid turned tumultuous—and periodically physically abusive. He went on a bender; I went from being his "*world in light*" to a girl expendable. Between Miller time and graduation, Jonathan said, "*After I get my diploma, there's nothing keeping me here.*" Ouch! Translation: "*Thanks for playing! Bye, Felicia!*" I knew I wouldn't have him forever, but I was a temptress and a fixer. I cajoled him with waterworks to stay. I hectored, hazed, henpecked him to choose me. I did untenable things to him—and his apartment—but for two years, I made no inroads in changing him or his mind. He left—no goodbye.

Jon met another Filipina—also a nurse—and married her.

Gold - the intrepid twenty-one year old I met on the Hoover Dam (*I, 26*). I was besotted the second I saw this *Braddah*. We had the kind of long distance relationship and intimacy you see in movies and read in novels. His love was the most tangible from any man I've ever met—and am likely to meet. For a conservative, Ben was my liberal adrenaline: I was a hermit, he, a ham; I was uptight, he, untamed; I was Calvin Coolidge taciturn, he, loquacious; I lived for later, he, for now with an aura of ease; bouncy, not bookish. Unabashed by his sexual proclivities and fraternity harem, Ben was so virile, he undressed me with his eyes. He held my hand, and I went bananas. He danced the haka; I was hypnotized. He pledged, *"Wherever you are, that's where I'll be."* Like teenagers, we had gobs of fun prancing in the D.C. nightlife, gallivanting around landmarks, backpacking from airport to airport, canoodling with calendars in tow, and being regular punters at *Nam-Viet*—just us, (*the late*) Donald Rumsfeld, and a fleet bodyguards triangulating the Phở diner. I galloped into this romance nostalgic from the last, so these getaways felt like going to the prom. Ben *was* the love of my life, my strongest weakness, my *Ku'uipo*. I thought he'd never be unfaithful, least of all on a drunken stupor; he thought he didn't need a venereal test drive—we were both horribly mistaken. Celibacy was sexual asbestos to his libido. I tried to neuter him monogamous. Make him honest, make him change, but this young lothario couldn't abstain from intercourse, even when he tried. Things went downhill pronto; the ejections from the emotional shrapnel were off the Richter scale. Stallion and I were irremediable. He freelanced, met a girl in Virginia, left her, pleaded I take him back over maudlin voicemails, but I brushed him off.

Ben U-turned to that Springfield girl and married her.

Trying to change someone wasn't an imprudent mistake I forgot I made, but one I never learned until I've overdone it thrice under the delusion that the first few were just tryouts, and that I'd get it right with repetition. If a boyfriend and a fiancé wouldn't change for me, maybe a husband would!

They needed *"saving,"* why not be Noah and build them an ark? Their edges were serrated, why not be Michelangelo and chisel them? Their lives were unformed, why not clear, brighten, and smooth their paths as if I were an antioxidant, antiaging facial serum? Why not? You don't fundamentally change someone you love, that's why!

"I love you, Bae! But I'll fundamentally change you!"

It's hubris!

Amid incompatibilities, I thought if I could make these men happy, they'd make me happier. If I loved harder, they'd try harder. If I remedied our incongruous worlds, we'd stay together. I thought I knew what was best for them and our relationships. With every hawkish attempt to change them, I overplayed my part, planted kernels of expectations, and mowed weeds of disenchantments. I told you, I'm a glutton for punishment and a sadistic overachiever.

These men had their own volition—none of them asked me to implement changes or infringe monopoly in their lives. They were making unsanitary choices, misapplying talents, living noxious lifestyles, and misusing time, but I couldn't repair what they didn't see as broken. It wasn't within my purview or power to solve *their* problems. It wasn't my job to make a project out of anyone or to turn boys into men. I couldn't entrench change upon those who didn't want it.

It took four men to teach me this one lesson. Two more, and I'll get a free mug.

Because I've excised myself from that varmint side of me I didn't want others to see and one I've fudged for eons to fix, I looked elsewhere to fix others. I made a compilation of their deficiencies, their rickety religions, their gelatinous morals, exhorted them to change for me and because of me, and fed myself emotionally on their impassioned, but half-assed efforts. Unmindful of my neediness to be of value, I wanted to be useful, to matter, and be *"the one"* to anyone.

Post hoc, I realized I was the trampoline who darted them to *"the one"* after me. It was I who changed into who they wanted me to be. I reshuffled my repertoire of ethics, and when you compromise one, you'll compromise the rest.

Do you know how quixotic it is to change people—against their will? Push a *"Pull"* door. Tickle a mannequin. Lick your elbow. Let me know how it goes.

In many of our relationships, we beaver away at changing what we don't like about others. We see the errors of their ways, don our Superman capes, turn into alchemists, and edify them to be better, refined people by tweaking their irksome mannerisms: leaving the toilet seat up; hoarding; burping; fibbing; and my anathema, audible gum chewing. If they dug their heels against our crusades, and little—if anything—changes, we entreat, redouble our efforts, maybe even sniffle and pout. We spin our wheels and get nowhere.

They're insoluble—we're fed up! We interlock our fingers, walk out, and hope *"It's my way or the highway"* would do the trick. Things then devolve into debacles.

Before you wring their necks, peddle your precepts to no avail, recommence this chimeric undertaking, or give up your firstborn to have them change, hit pause.

In her TEDx talk, Harvard professor Dr. Tali Sharot said, *"If you threatened people, if fear is induced, it will get them to act. And it seems like a really reasonable assumption, except for the fact that science shows that warnings have very limited impact on behavior."*

You could generate discussions by wielding dominion over someone's behavior, but do you see any follow up actions? Unceasing, unremitting, bona fide actions? Lackadaisical efforts are insignificant. Passing promises are indicative of nothing. Inconsistent and intermittent trials do not count. Stepping up then slipping up doesn't either.

And don't even get me started with intentions—intentions without demonstrations are like lamps without lightbulbs.

If they scoff at your proffer, balk at your advice, or your ultimatum can't make them say goodbye to their old ways, these aren't necessarily pointers that warrant a repeat or new stratagems. If dragooned, they may change, but not in ways you'd find cogent. The more you badger or bribe, the more they'll pull back. It forges a cycle of frustration and pain, and you—in all likeness—will be left disaffected.

Still insistent on remolding someone?

When was the last time someone tried to change you? Did you wish they'd just love, respect, and accept you as you are and where you are in life? Did you continue living your life with your inveterate routines? Or did you change just long enough to keep them around?

When was the last time you tried to change yourself? Snuff out a nasty habit? How easy was the improvisation of the *"new you"*? Past behaviors are best predictors of future ones, so did temptations divert your progress?

I'm not saying people cannot change. We *can*! If history's any indication, you see every form of life underpins one of the most—if not the best substantiated theories: evolution. You and I and every complex creature are humdingers of such adaptation.

Big picture: it's not about your impetus to change them; it's about their impetus to change themselves. Their destinies are theirs to decide, not yours to dictate. You don't override their choices, and I don't get to overturn them, even if they get your panties all in a wad, and even if—this is harsh, so brace yourself—those choices don't include you.

> *"What is necessary to change a person is to change his awareness of himself."* - Abraham Maslow

Sounds like a holistic and appropriate approach to me!

Tell them your concerns, offer love and support, print yourself a copy of *The Serenity Prayer*, then leave them to their own ways. They'll clean up their acts one way or another. In time, you'll see them rehabilitated on Tinder, married on Instagram, crowing about their new family, trumpeting job promotions on LinkedIn, or engaged on Facebook, talking like a grown-up, praising God with a genteel vocabulary.

Then refract your light inward.

> *"Everyone thinks of changing the world, but no one thinks of changing himself."* - Leo Tolstoy

Never was this more clear than when I evaluated my part of the problem and asked myself why I participated in these changing games with men indisposed to play. My pursuit was more than wanting to see how far my tentacles could extend, more than overreaching to redo their lives, more than needing to be useful. I needed control in all its forms.

I parsed my problems and their paramount participants, and guess who was at the pith of it all? Drumroll, please! I'll give you a hint: it starts with a "*J*" and ends with a "*G*."

> *"All the world's a stage, and all the men and women merely players."* - William Shakespeare

You're not meant to be a footnote in someone else's cast of characters. Shift your awareness in and towards your self-understanding. You can prop others—not change them—once you've fulfilled yourself. Lead your own life; that's your role. Those supporting actors have their own. Reprise and compose your script without rewriting theirs.

II – RED FLAGS

"The greater danger for most of us lies not in setting our aim too high and falling short; but in setting our aim too low, and achieving our mark."
- Michelangelo

4. EYE OF THE STORM

"Don't be afraid to give up the good to go for the great."
- John D. Rockefeller

Dasies are my favorite flowers, yellow roses second, phalaenopsis orchids third. During our courtship, Carlos showered me with floral arrangements and hand-drawn artwork of our names, canvased with ribbons, hearts, and glitters. I was deluged with restaurant receipts, primitive gestures of handwritten love letters on my pillow, *"I miss you"* on coffee sleeves, *"You're the love of my life"* calligraphies, trunks of missives, and sappy Post-it on a Tupper-ware, on the fridge, on the bathroom mirror, and a butterfly figurine to add to my Baccarat Papillons. I rarely had emotional exposure with my preceding boyfriends, and even rarer did I parcel shiny ornaments to them. Kleenex is for the soupy; Hallmark and Pixar are too touchy-feely.

What I lacked in cheesy familiarity, he compensated for in mushiness. I'd tell you more, but I'd barf.

From the start, I couldn't imagine what he saw in me.

I'm nuttier than a bag of walnuts. Cynical, morose, stroppy, sarcastic. I'm frozen in the 60's boho bandanas, bouffant, rotary phones, vintage teapots and scarves, the 70's kaftans, 80's tunes, and the 90's supermodel makeup. I snort when I laugh and fidget during dates. A workaholic klutz wearing brooches and scrunchies, a goody-two-shoes with a chubby waistline, and a prudish maiden who loves documentaries, hates subtitles, played the flute, never smoked a Molly, and wanted to be a monastic nun in high school (*yes, I'm boring and bizarre*). I don't come with baggage; I have cargoes.

Ravenous for love, I trekked through crevices, caverns, and catacombs to find it. Men vied for my attention, but no one had embodied a trinity of character, humility, and integrity or reflected my reverence for the spirit world and my own complexity, idiosyncrasies, and attentiveness. A loner who lives vividly in the metaphysical, revels in Mother Earth's munificence, and seeks meaning and purpose. Objective in logic, subjective in values. A champion for the indigents and the downtrodden. Someone acerbic, but wouldn't walk on eggshells around me, and an old soul with warmth and sensitivity. Intuitive and elusive. Altruistic and arcane.

I rolled the dice of love frantically trawling for such a man, but no luck. Those I found held my heart in their hands and returned it bleeding—one gut-wrenching, bone-crushing breakup after another. Histories of heartaches taught me to never, ever glide towards the guardrails.

In distrust of all men for the misdeeds of a few, a good man had to be a phantasm, so I stopped believing in one.

I stopped believing—period.

Then I met Carlos. He had *none* of the above criteria, but he said all the right things: he said I was beauty and brains; he said he didn't have to drink to tolerate me; he said he'd insert himself into the underworld; he said he'd lock up the grifters to protect me and others from impious acts; he said *"You're the best thing that ever happened to me. Te amo con todo mi corazon."* I felt unhinged, unwanted, unloved, but he didn't share my disparaging views. He said I was his world; the fulfillment of his hopes and dreams. He said nothing was above me, and no one would come after me.

Furthermore, he also declared, *"I would never hurt you."*

C'mon in, Ms. Garcia—the water's fine!

The prodromal signs: our distinctly dissimilar life stages; unrelated personalities and passions; chasms between his imprecise goals and my unambiguous ambitions; and his past was as horrid as my own. But I wanted romance redux!

He was a bloviating Millennial, borderline cocky, facetious, untutored, criminally versatile (*if you know what I mean*), and his jokes were annoying, but he could also be a peach! So, I drank as much fantasy potions to get me tipsy and dolled myself up with love goggles and rose-tinted glasses to look beyond our imbalances.

From the outset, Carlos was persistent, and he pursued me doggedly. It was nonplussing, but also astoundingly sweet. I was shattered, but he was an indefatigable *"Mexi-Can"* with motor skills to fix anything—hey, he could fix me! By golly, I thought he could part the Red Sea! I was too self-deprecating to believe other-wise. He was my Tarzan; the apparition of *La Virgen de Guadalupe* who'd snatch me from the chancy currents of singlehood.

Carlos made me feel like the most bodacious woman in the room—making him an overqualified suitor. It wasn't so much a question of why this varsity jock would give me the time of day, but a fear that any other man would not.

Even so, we cohabited inverse of one another, and as soon as he moved in, a potpourri of sensory changes aerated the house. *Fabuloso,* fabric softeners, cilantro, and the enticing aromas of his meal preps—the latter by far was the most fragrant of all. Carlos refinished and remodeled with new furnishings and appliances. Aesthetically, it thawed out my unwelcomingly minimalist home, but appearance could not alter the reality of our immense mismatch.

The kitchen—I couldn't gloat there. I knew squat about this witchcraft called *"cooking."* I had no set of knives, no pots and pans, salt or pepper—not even a houseplant. My oven was a warehouse of souvenirs, trinkets, and bins. Whatever I *"homemade"* was either overcooked or inedible, but he was domestically superb. He had the skillset for Michelin rating churros, chile relleño, blueberry emoji pancakes, fajitas, quesadillas, enchiladas, and strawberry tamales!

The sack—I was inept there, too. Carlos would be my first, and he said I'd be his last.

The television—the first thing he hauled in when he moved in was his gigantic flat screen—suitcases, toothbrush, and other daily requisites came later. My Mum had loathed TV since I was a chipmunk. To her, it was a learning retardant and a passive hobby that stifled a child's imagination, so she banned it and had me read and do crosswords instead. I bought my first TV for the 2008 inauguration—a bunny-eared, boxed model for $20 from Craigslist. After freezing like a popsicle at the National Mall, I watched the news at home and never again turned it on.

Carlos minced his words. I'm unconcerned if you aspirate on mine.

He was perceptible. I'm a woman of many contradictions. An enigma and a paradox even to myself. I can slit you with my truculent tongue this second, snog with you the next. I'm a docile flower and an ornery blade intermingled into one. Tremendously withdrawn, but a cut-throat with a resting bitch face. Chipper if recognized, but gauche when noticed. I love helping, but requesting help isn't my forte.

Those who know me—or think they do—say I come across as inflexible, icy, and intimidating, but I'm a real softie. An oddball! Carlos said he loved that about my personality—all ten of them.

With my terry pajamas, Dora the Explorer hairdo, Steve Urkel bifocals, and body pillow, I read voraciously. My godmother's library was my daycare, where I doodled and had unlimited VIP access to encyclopedias.

He was easygoing. I overthink. Overanalyze. Over worry. If around buffoons, my patience and attention short circuit. He didn't use ciphers. I speak in the vernacular; I think in metaphors, My e-mails are essays, my writing, periphrastic and allegoric. Their subliminal messages are perspicacious only to a few.

He was "*DFW*" - down for whatever. I'm uber systematic. Stuff doesn't haphazardly happen around me, not if it's my purpose. *"I exercise control in all things,"* like dominatrix protagonist Christian Grey *(nothing kinky)*, and like titular CIA assassin Jason Bourne, *"I "don't do random. There's always an objective."*

Every move has an import or intent.

Carlos had sporadic déjà vu. I live inside my head with an eidetic memory, encrypted analogies, allusions, homonyms, and palindromes. My brainbox has subfloors; I toggle there between five tabs of self-improvement, throw-backs, future situations, hypothetical conversations, and poetries, and I multitask with idealism and philosophies. On a first date, I don't think about a second date, instead I wonder if you're agnostic, do you believe in the sanctity of life, what makes you tick, do you have a liturgy of baseline values, do you respect women of all political affiliations, and together, can we eradicate cruelty, prejudice, and illiteracy?

However oblivious I may seem, I notice *everything*.

Carlos' zests in life were the gym, the San Francisco 49ers, and the Boston Red Sox. Foreplay for me is an all-nighter exchange of songs and lyrics with someone I love.

I can listen to a song a billion times, but not once had I said "*I love you*" first—Carlos did it for me.

He accepted all my craziness without discord.

When I'm with a man, I'm in one of two positions: aloof or freefalling into love—no moderation. When I'm in, I'm all in, but I have an on-and-off switch between irrelevance and love—no in between. My sanctum's rigged with padlocks and firewalls—trust is the access key. If betrayed, I slam the door unceremoniously, and those serpents are eternally uninvited. I obfuscate when I'm nervous, withdraw when I'm hurt or vulnerable, and recoil when irate or inundated. My lockdowns are protracted—if not indefinite.

But Carlos' patience was prodigious, and so was mine.

Coming in at 110 pounds of pre-existing fear, I'm a counter puncher. I do *not* initiate anything until I feel safe. Placid but not pliable, I wait for you to make the first move. By keeping you (*and everyone*) at arm's length, I can parry an uppercut. I slither in an inch after you step up a mile, close enough for an intimate interchange, but far enough from a defensive blow. A tactical jab against a romantic knockout.

I'm an introvert; crowds drain me. He was my extroverted counterpart; social gatherings charged his internal battery. Fluent in Spanish, Portuguese, English, and smooth talk, he could start a conversation with anyone, anytime, anywhere. With an eerie flair for non-verbal cues, I blend in and adapt like a chameleon, read between the lines, decode abstracts, and hear what is not being said.

Would he end my independent streak? My solo outings? *Nunca.* He said he'd long favored cougars. Conflicts (*still*) ranked high among the most anaphylactic of my allergies, so to fend them off, there was a phrase we forbade each other from saying—it'd be blasphemy if we did. Premarital sex was barred, but he didn't grouse—that was alien to me.

The unequivocal disqualifier: to parent or not to parent? I was dead set on not having children that it ossified into this non-negotiable deal breaker. I didn't prevaricate. I wanted a partner who'd make this choice *with* me, never *for* me, because to ask a man to sacrifice his happiness for my own gain would be egotistically vile and downright iniquitous.

We had—what I thought—were unhypocritical discussions, and I was convinced Carlos also did not want children. We were on the same non-parental page.

Carlos then asked me to marry him—in Spanish.

G-O-A-L!

How could I resist the alluring benefits of marriage that had beckoned me when I'd been on the wife waitlist since I was eighteen? Love had long evaded me since; I didn't want to lose this slot! I was a thirty-two-year-old single nomad still living in the hangover of my ex—pinning for him. I was in like with Carlos; I was (*still*) in love with Ben.

It's time. Carlos was the one—he *had* to be. I kept saying it to myself until I believed it or take what's behind door #2: end up alone, looking for the needle in the haystack. I'll take "*A proxy will do for now*" for $900, Alex. Plus I was too dinged up to repel what he proposed—in any language.

I was a damsel in distress; he was a blowhard machismo. What could possibly go wrong?

I wanted to bolt on the eve of the wedding, but didn't have the cojones to slink out. May 5, 2011. The waterfall of the Hilton Hawaiian Village was a semblance of Eden, and the frills of the Ocean Crystal Chapel were iridescent. Thirty-eight families and friends from Orange County and around the D.C. beltway were enfolded by modern elegance.

My best friend Jeremy, a naval officer, flew in from Japan just to give me away. For seventeen years after and during his senior year at the U.S. Naval Academy, he'd signed off his letters and postcards with "*Think of me.*" After a sweet embrace, Jeremy whispered, "*Think of—him.*"

It was too late to turn the ship around.

The doors opened to the death knell of *"Ave Maria."* I had a rosary in one hand, a hideous broccoli bouquet in another. Scuffing my feet down the aisle, my steps felt cumbersome. There was Carlos at the alter—my matrimonial guillotine. A Ti leaf lei was around his collar. His face was aglow, his smile, beatific. His persistence had paid off.

I looked at this man and pictured the face of another. He wiped my tear with a handkerchief as the chaplain orbed us with a *Lazo de Novia*. Our sacrament, as engraved on *his* ring, was *"Para Siempre."*

I had walked into my own execution.

Carlos changed into his guayabera, and I harnessed all the strength I could to keep up my pantomime performance for our oceanfront luau at The Bayer Estate in Āina Haina (*the McGarrett home in Hawaii Five-O*). It was so sumptuous, even I started to believe it was real.

He slept like a baby in a manger postcoital; my untrodden territory of thirty-two years was untrodden no more.

In my eyes, this was only a marriage in writing, but after saying, *"I do,"* I realized what I just did. What a morass I'd gotten myself into? And my husband…

By twilight, my on-screen persona was done emoting. I sat at our hotel's lanai, gawping at my husband, thinking this was no less his fault than mine. Carlos didn't hold me at gunpoint—no one did. Much to my friends' disbelief and my mother's dismay, I signed on the dotted line. I could've been a runaway bride with every reason for calling it off, but it was inexorable. I transferred my hope for happiness and hung my entire future on the shoulders of a boy who talked a good game.

I'm accountable for this tempest and the extent to which it would condemn me into self-made captivity.

Many remembered our nuptial and our marriage so much more beautifully than the truth would've suggested they should. They've dubbed us as *"the perfect couple,"* but we were the perfect storm.

5. TROUBLE IN PARADISE

"And the day came when the risk to remain tight in a bud was more painful than the risk it took to blossom."
- Anaïs Nin

A conglomeration of factors, downturns, and travails imperiled my marriage to its inevitable stalemate. My ex-husband and I, we were never of one body. Even those closest to me could only decipher a mite of my mind and grapple a portion of my heart; he did neither. Our unalike personalities and malignant prognosis predated our freshman year as man and wife. For the sake of brevity, the shambles through which we fought to keep our vows, the indiscretions that beset our union, and the jeremiad of its terminal phase won't be rehashed here. The maelstroms are too convoluted for a rundown, too piteous to be shared, and too painful for a play-by-play. I could archive the top three and list a half dozen more, but they'd better off quarantined within my memory.

We've entered into a covenant together, and together we've contributed to its demise. The good, the bad, the best, the worst—we had them. Every day that passed, I shrank and faded into my husband. From where I stand, the best of me wasn't enough, and my all wasn't either. In contrition, I'd claimed the blame for my offenses and deservedly so.

In the wee hours of July 16, 2017, Carlos' friend asked me a plainspoken question, but not so plain as I was overawed. *"What would you do if another man came along?"*

My barbican suddenly felt like plexiglass with this man. I answered, but stuttered. He saw through me, through the charade. At the apogee of despair, I prayed for someone—anyone—to come along and fetch me. That or an asteroid to pounce me out of my misery.

Within a month, my Mum sent me a letter addressed to "*Lyn*," my familial nickname. I thought it was another one of her rigmaroles about how I splatted her dream of having a pilot or a physician for a son-in-law by marrying Carlos (*you see why I never confided to her?*), but I was off-target.

To translate from Tagalog, she asked, "*Until when are you going to sacrifice?*" "*Did you become happy?*" and "*Why do you need to suffer?*" Her antenna was *that* high—must be the maxim, "*A mother knows best.*" Mum wrote, not in subtlety or exaggeration, but of the truth, and she'd blessed with her full throttle support.

Unbeknown to me, Mum's maternal instinct had kept her abreast from six thousand miles away. She'd known that I'd been on the divorce runaround for over six years. I kept telling myself I'd retry to leave my husband "*later.*" Mum thought it's been long enough.

In October 2011, five months into our marriage, I asked for a divorce. In tears and on bended knees, Carlos begged me to reconsider, but I refused. He knew I wasn't bluffing. After two days of unbearable silence, a beaker smashed in the kitchen and portended my greatest fear: Carlos "*fell and hit [his] head.*" An unwitnessed fall *without* a hematoma, a fracture, or cerebral ischemia. The hospital neurologist saw *nothing*. Carlos feigned amnesia from this "*brain injury,*" and he'd forgotten *everything*: his family; his childhood; our wedding; and me—his wife.

But he did say, "*Don't tell my grandma.*"

Needless to say, what kind of wife would I'd been had I left my husband in *that* condition? A mixture of *The Vow* and *50 First Dates*. Carlos needed me, and for the next six and a half years, everything stopped. EVERYTHING.

It was incontestable that I couldn't just walk away from this marriage—I had to illude my way out of it. That was the cliffhanger; the scam on which the façade of this telenovela was built.

Same bullshit ballgame, but with extra innings.

What's the first rule of military combat? One I enacted in my second attempt to freedom. Never reveal your position. A silent move is the most efficient one. I had a double life during my undercover operation. A deceiving diversion to con Carlos into believing I wasn't going to leave him—not anymore. To download my new identity, I withdrew from families, friends, and colleagues whose interests, personas, and enterprises were enormously antithetical to those of my husband's and homogenized myself with his cronies—none of whom were in my age cohort. They were affable, but some were unrefined. Their energies were different, their discussions, pablum. If pensive conversations were brain food, I was mentally malnourished.

I didn't morph into a happy wife; I masqueraded as one.

The bustling inner bowels of Washington D.C. made me senile and Carlos cranky. We felt gelded. Did we want to get pared down by another subzero winter? I have Postural Orthostatic Syndrome (*POTS*), and with the locale's hectic lifestyle, I got increasingly symptomatic. Each gripe called for a relocation—someplace to *"hang loose"* with maximal sunlight, Hapa, Bob Marley, and unbelievable ambiance.

I suggested Hawaii, and Carlos assented with ardor. We left D.C. on April 24, 2013. I had ulterior motives.

Hawaii was a strategic move, but not at all confounding. We did, in fact, got hitched there! He would undoubtedly ask for alimony—maybe permanently with his *"disability."* I own a property in D.C., but Hawaii's family court doesn't like to play realtor, and alimony is anomalously conferred to less than 9% of its divorces. It's a no-fault state, and a six-month separation period is unrequired, unlike D.C.

There'd been trouble in paradise for years.

I didn't want another six months of playacting—even a day of it made my stomach churn. I could *not* wait. I would *not* wait. Six months: another unproven, inopportune accident could happen in six months; another unwitnessed, amnesia aggravated *"brain injury"* could happen in six months.

His own sister Paloma thought he was faking it!

Belatedly, I wondered if he knew I was *never* in love with him? Was he so blithely bamboozled that I wasn't going anywhere? I kept my eye on the ball and maintained the status quo, but I was no Sally Fields—I was not *that* good. Moot point now.

My shark of a lawyer knew **my meticulously laid out exit logistics were spin-offs of my last,** and our collaboration had be copacetic and furtive. What would take years, he had to do in months. I saw my window, and it was razor thin. *"I'm not getting trapped again. This could be my last-ditch effort."* This time around, I had patience, planning, and prayers, but no intimating, and no warming.

In outwitting my spouse, I learned from the best.

Fast forward to September 23, 2017. I told Carlos I was leaving him—again. *"I'm sorry I had to do it this way, Carlos, but I didn't want you to have another brain injury."*

Stupefied, Carlos knew he couldn't sidestep this divorce or piggyback any more subterfuge to his prior forestalling.

Not *this* time.

"I see it in your eyes. I know you're done," he said.

What was less overt, given my standoffish countenance, was that my heart was throbbing, ready to rupture had he played hardball, but he was cooperative. He wanted to sign the papers right there and then without skimming a page, but I thought it'd be sporting to give him time to peruse the decree and ingest the dissolution of our marriage without distraction. We amicably went our separate ways. I went to my Mum's hotel; he walked back to our apartment.

Before reconvening the next morning, I updated those I considered closest to us and broke the news to Hawaii, then Philippines, then bicoastal.

I've asked *"The Troops"* to *"NOT post anything on social media regarding this private matter, please… meanwhile, we appreciate having true friends at a difficult time like this."* I learned three things once rosy times were over: some took my message to heart; some were unreceptive to my words; and my last sentence was premature.

Without dickering over child custody or the title to my house (*hedged solely under my name*), we should part on neutral grounds with minimum to no fuzz. I'd kept up with the car's payments, so we could sell it. This wouldn't be a production. My offer was more than middling.

Carlos would leave the marriage with more than what he entering it—which was close to nothing. But he declined. He was adamant. He wanted more—preposterously more.

To paraphrase my chaffer:

"You know you're not the only one who's going from a two-income household to a single-income, right?"

He was unmoved.

"You know I'm supporting my family in the Philippines, and a $2,250 rent to pay on my own now, and my D.C. mortgage, and my lawyer fees, and my student loans."

He was stoic. He wanted two years of upkeep.

"And you want me to pay you $1,000 a month on top of all of that. For two years? That's too much! Do you plan to work? I know you're going to live with your mother."

He didn't budge.

"How about for a year? $1,000 a month for a year. That's $12,000. I've supported myself, and us, and my family with much less before."

He still didn't budge.

"That's $24,000! On top of the car! In addition to the money you'll get once you sign! Do you know how much money that is? Have you had that much money?"

"About half of that," he said.

He was so nonchalant, and I fretted with rancor! This leech wanted more than what I brought to the table—I bought that fucking table! Now he'd offload his responsibilities to me with piles of *my* cash!

A few days after our lopsided mediation, he said, *"My mom told me I can go after half of your condo's interest, but I won't. I know you'll fight for that."* As if I'd take him or his mother at their word.

My 401K and the interest on my condo during the marriage were *"both on the line."* He was legally entitled to half of the first and the entirety of the latter. Knowing this, he had a trump card with nothing to lose—no assets. He could take his time negotiating and squandering more of mine. I could rescind my offer, but he could take this production to court and have a judge decide—until debt do us part.

"You could pay him or you could pay me. I'm on your side either way," my lawyer said. *"He hit the jackpot when he married you, kid. You can give him what he wants, take the hit now, recover later."*

A losing battle; I was too tired to duke it out. My financial indemnities were ransomed. I acquiesced and threw money at the problem forthwith, plus a surcharge. Forget fairness. Better an unequal resolution than a suspended one.

For the second time in this relationship, I settled. I settled to stay in it, and I settled to get out.

To encapsulate: Carlos was absolved from over $7,000 of amassed marital debt; he received a padded $3,000 for just signing the papers; and he got the SUV, bundled with two years of a monstrously oversize $1,000 per month support for the sum of $24,000 from 2018 through 2019.

What did I get? My life back. And a galleon of debt.

On November 14, 2017, the anniversary of our first date, I sent him the divorce decree imprinted with three signatures:

his; mine; and the judge named David. With those names, my marriage was over. The divorce was final.

Following our fallout, I tried to be cordial with Carlos, but I couldn't be diplomatic in my attempts. I couldn't tolerate or treat him with the civility of a stranger. Over the coming months, I became more furious at him. Never before had I felt this financially extorted. I was enraged at the fact that some make disproportionate sacrifices while others skate through life. But more, something inside me died with the divorce: respect.

Knowing him, I worried askance that he'd leave the island and finagle the car with him—with my name still on it. My lawyer fueled my mental wildfire, *"The main concern is for you to be off the debt... if he hits or kills somebody, you could still have liability."*

Then there were the nosy outsiders with an aversion to the truth gurgling diatribes and obscenities at me and about me on social media—protesting on Carlos' behalf. He assured me he'd *"make sure to convey the message to everyone,"* and he'd *"make sure they don't bother"* me again. Carlos gave me his word, but in shunning me while spreading lies, shacking up, and giving free rides to these assholes, he later attested it had no worth.

Falsus in uno, falsus in omnibus.

The enmity wasn't uneven. It was no lover's tiff. War was waged, and both our claws came out. The situation didn't bring out the best of me. I can laugh now at how I terribly mischanneled my anger, LOL! You can take the girl out of Baltimore, but... Ya feeling me? This vigilante artiste put on a hoodie, bused it to Walmart, and got herself stencils, superglue, and spray paint—lots of spray paint—and went gangster on that car!

I'll show you *"cray-cray"*!

All my suspicions materialized as 2017 drew to a close.

Carlos left Hawaii, absconded the car, ignored all my calls, texts, and e-mails, and resurfaced in February 2018 asking for—wait for it—his money. He did write, *"If I don't need [your] money anymore I'll let you know."* To this present day (*even after his "change of circumstance"*), I never got that memo.

I was brining in the aftermath of my divorce bedlam. I was ambulanced for arrhythmias and angina. An airstrike of animosities, including but not limited to egregious gossips, betrayals, and misguided loyalties sniped me into the new year. At a crossroads, friends were centrifuged from foes, and I made less of them than enemies.

My life had whirred into a tailspin.

III – BLACKOUT

"Even the darkest night will end and the sun will rise."
- Victor Hugo

6. PULL THE PLUG

"You can't go back and change the beginning, but you can start where you are and change the ending."
- C.S. Lewis

Unreasonable expectations, overkill bickering, lack of commitment—these and more are the bevy of reasons why approximately 50% of marriages in America deadlocks in separation or divorce—that's one divorce per thirteen seconds. And the other 50%? Are they happy? Are they defying the odds or confined to conjugal manacles, affrighted to jump ship? Did they go in for the right reasons and stay for the wrong ones?

It got me thinking about settling and starting over.

Who among us is plodding away, past the plateaus of our jumbo scale slipups and granular glitches? We swan dive into epic projects, and if they fall by the wayside, we noose ourselves from shutting them down and switching gear. Flared up with frustration and regrets, we trudge through a sclerotic academic career to not lose our tenure. We finish an uninteresting book because we're already fifty pages in (*not this one, right?*). We perseverate with more energy, more time, more supplemental over-head into businesses that misfire with galactic turnovers and inefficient revenue.

Wanting to pull the plug on my marriage before it was even officiated, I didn't think I'd stay in it for seven days, yet I prolonged it by seven years. By then, I—we—have already invested so much in the life we've built, and I was a portly, deflowered, rundown, thirty-nine-year-old Grinch without a fallback, should I tumble after a quantum leap. Who would want me then? And what Catholic strata would welcome an ex-communicant bearing the scarlet letter "*D*"? Divorced.

Everything I've become was a far cry from the filly I once had been, but beehives of single ladies pray for the "*Mrs.*" prefix, so although my marriage—tedium and all—was less than I hoped for, it was more than I deserved. The hazards of stepping into the wilderness, unmarried and unaided, were too dicey, and going off on a tangent could ricochet, so discouraged by both—and without the temerity to do either—I plugged away at my doomed dreams and waited for an oracle, an actuary, or a burning bush to tell me when it'd be safe to embark on an extemporaneous venture.

In the meantime, I tried in vain to mold a nonevent into something it wasn't and could never be. I dithered around without an endgame in sight—not even a transit for years to come—and clutched to my opened can of worms because if I were to walk away, I'd be uncovering a new one. Better a wasteland I knew than one I didn't. I settled in my setback because a retraction felt wasteful after all the time, energy, money, and efforts I spent staying in it, and I'd rather forgo my happiness than accept my ills. I held on to a mistake because I've spent so much time making it.

But at the nadir of despondency, I asked myself if living a life in the doldrum was any different from being dead.

Got dead plants you keep watering? It's going nowhere for months, even years, but you can't stop digging in the name of finding the metaphorical or proverbial gold? Is intuition telling you to chart a new territory, but fear is impeding you on its helm? Trying to move forward with a failure??

How's that working for you?

Economists call this decision making bias *"The sunk cost fallacy."* We rationalize misspent resources on endeavors that aren't coming to fruition instead of cutting our losses. Wary of revocation, we continue to underwrite them as we miss out on opportunities by chasing profits that will never come to pass—making big mistakes exponentially bigger.

I was once gouged to finish a salty, $23 crab soup. I had flank pain, hypertension, and pitting edema. Where was the logic in my inference? I couldn't repossess my money, but the inflammation, indigestion, elevated blood pressure, and aching were avoidable—if only I focused on future cost.

To my compatriots of tenacity, I know we don't like to bid good riddance to our goals or part ways with loved ones.

But where is the honor of going down with a sinking ship? The future is what matters, where salient resources must be redeployed. We can't envisage tomorrow's possibilities by making choices based on yesterday's remorse. Nugatory mementos and memories can often make your fear of a new frontier greater than today's reality.

I'm *not* enjoining you to cut the cord to your consortium or repeal your marriage (*or any ties*) or make any alternative arrangement in your life. I'm not Nostradamus, and I won't pretend to be one.

You know who and what's wreaking havoc in your life and what's in the rearview mirror. You know which disaster(s) you keep dipping in because you've poured so much blood, sweat, and tears into it. You know when enough is enough, when to call the time of death, and disembark.

Until then (*if you're on a limbo*), reexamine the truth with your eyes on tomorrow's hopes and not on today's hurdles.

You have inalienable rights to life, liberty, and the pursuit of happiness. You may be in the pregame of your pinnacle. Satisfaction, joy, peace, passion could be on the other side of goodbye. At first, equilibrium will be disrupted—even disarranged—but the crucible of a shipwreck could be the springboard from past losses to potential gains—not just in dividends—but in all kinds of benedictions.

So your dreams (*and mine*) splattered like embers. Must you throw what's left of them into the pyre? Why not let bygones be bygones? Your self-inflicted point of no return is a checkmate of what was, not a vista of what is and what can be. Reflect on your own sunk costs and the pros and cons associated with staying and going. Failures have no refunds or barters, but not everything you lose is a loss.

Repeat after me: Not everything you lose is a loss.

If your gold standard is sequel after sequel of sunken costs, resuming relationships beyond repair, dilly-dallying with makeshift dealings and unfruitful careers, or yenning for new and enthusiastic segments in life, but you're diddling at a layover, believing it's your final destination, or if your gold standard is anything less than the actualization of your best self, how about going platinum?

Maybe you're at half-time or on the cusp of a windfall. Maybe where you are now is only a precursor to something eminent, but you're too afraid of the unexplored. Fear is the thief of all hopes, but courage is the prerequisite. You'll need courage to have any hope of prospering, awareness to discern when it's time to move on, and maturity to own a mistake without being held hostage to it.

I've roamed around the wrong roadways for years, fretted it was too late to change my course of action, flummoxed if I stay a little longer and try a little harder, there might just be a bonanza to rake in or a prize to claim—all in that order. After divorce, I thought the world would either be a jungle or a drought. One miscalculated blip and whoops! There'd be nothing for me to till. I thought if my marriage croaked, so would I.

What a scarce mentality to handicap oneself.

I bewail giving my ex-husband the best of me, but as for the rest of me?

I want to behold the Colosseum, the Giza pyramids, Petra, Machu Picchu, Christ the Redeemer, Chichen Itza; go to Nepal for Holi; eat tapas at Barcelona bistros, mezzes in Athens, and risotto at a Venice trattoria; stay at an Aspen chalet; ramp up my subpar Italian; rove around the Eiffel Tower with Mum; see the Louvre; gulp baguettes, falafels, eclairs, croissants, and Parisian coffee; stopover at Capri; dance the Argentine tango; learn to whistle and ride a bike.

Divorce destabilized my friendships, my finances, my faith, but He told not to fear, three-hundred-and-sixty-five times.

> *"Be still, and know that I am God."*
> \- Psalm 46:10

I've emptied out my cup and trusted His prescient word.

In my willingness to die in *every* way I was before, I made myself available to His bounty and to unfold into who I'm becoming. He'd brought me this far, and he's not letting go now. He never will.

Your life is your manuscript.

> *"Don't be afraid to make some edits."*
> \- Business baron Richard Branson

If you're waffling with one foot out, one foot in, Godspeed. Win, lose, or draw, may you be reawakened and sanguine about the possibilities of new beginnings because the only palisades are the ones you put in place. The cost you might pay for the rest of your life may not be the pain of holding on, but the regret of not letting go.

> *"For what it's worth: it's never too late or, in my case, too early to be whoever you want to be. There's no time limit, stop whenever you want. You can change or stay the same, there are no rules to this thing. We can make the best or the worst of it. I hope you make the best of it. And I hope you see things that startle you. I hope you feel things you never felt before. I hope you meet people with a different point of view. I hope you live a life you're proud of. If you find that you're not, I hope you have the courage to start all over again."*
> - F. Scott Fitzgerald

7. LIGHTS OUT

"You are so brave and quiet I forget you are suffering."
- Ernest Hemmingway

Going to the principal's office was a recurring event for me in elementary school, and so were visiting Mrs. Turner's office—my English teacher. On a frosty afternoon in 1989, my parents and I had a meeting with her, and she regurgitated the same searing remarks she'd been harping since I matriculated: I was an awkward schoolgirl; a mousy immigrant; and a wallflower without a seedling talent or a penchant for learning and acculturating to America. Those were only preliminary proclamations; wait for her awful closing statement.

My father wanted a precocious child, but got me instead.

Mrs. Turner's final remark was a pitchfork into his dream. It was a potent shot of criticism, even for a class dummy like me.

"Jodelene cannot write a sentence."

Like a scythe through grass, her words lanced a chunk of my eleven-year-old heart. I felt worthless.

After we adjourned in chilling silence—a language spoken fluently at home—my father walked down the corridors wearing a heavy corona of disappointment, so much so, he couldn't look at me.

Millions of Filipinos had scampered to the U.S. to enrich their lives, and my folks dotted every I's and crossed every T's to legally petition this dreamer. Naturalized at birth, many were jealous of my American citizenship. To them, it was the Mayflower that sailed me to my storybook chateau and chariots, but the wanderlust was a stench underground of secrets—all of which was the worst kind to have.

I was a newcomer; a fish out of water. Impressionable, shy, artless—all the qualities my father frowned upon. Though reunited with my Mum, our closeness couldn't protect me. In fact, she couldn't protect me from many things. I didn't want to study or mingle. I wanted to go back to the family I left behind and not feel so inapposite. Life with them was good. Life with my parents was accursed.

Outside the ramparts of the hellhole we called *"home"* were mountains of misunderstandings about the tailored images and cushy life of what was, in fact, a gilded cage.

At first glance, I'm the mockup of the biblical child Isaac, the promised offspring, born into privilege. But by contrast, I'm akin to Ishmael, the disadvantaged son, born out of sin. I'm a child of incest, spurned as a mistake, an anomaly, a bastard, an outcast.

My birth was the genesis of the cold war between the Delos Reyes and the patriarchs, the Garcias. As my father's only heir, they thought I'd parlay myself into an inheritance, and my mother would swindle them out of their endowment. Incensed over the scandal, fearing they'd be overpowered by an infant (*that'd be me*), they dispossessed me and *mi madre* of everything—much as Ishmael and his ostracized mother Hagar were uprooted without a penny to their name.

The next seven years, the two household saga simmered to new heights, widening the divide with no rapprochement—ever. My father knew of our exile, but chose to disappear and be uninvolved. Before I turned seven, we met.

I learned of my father's power at once, and so promptly did he start making changes—starting with my name. I was no longer Darlene Delos Reyes; I became Jodelene Garcia.

He said he'd keep Mum and me safe, and take good care of us, just as he'd done with the rest of the Garcia family as their enthroned breadwinner. I trusted him. He was Daddy Warbucks—so I thought.

But he made no pretense of propitiating. In a brief length of time, it became lucid that life with him was no fairy tale—not without its downsides.

With a sterling reputation in our community, he had ties to Filipino bigwigs. They could never fathom his licentious morale and wouldn't want to even if they could. Trussed in lavish finery at quadrilles or dressed in dominance at home, he had to be the main attraction. The Prefect—never to be outshined. Omniscient, intractable, one part Don Corleone, two parts Lucifer.

This was just the tip of the iceberg.

When he booted me out with Mum at the vertex of winter, like a landlord evicting his tenants, forcing us to live at her boss' facility, he must've forgotten we were his family.

When he scrunched his knuckles and pummeled the wall within an inch of Mum's face to stop her from whimpering, he must've forgotten she was his wife.

When he chased me with a butcher's knife, slapped me on the right, then backhanded by a left into days of catatonic silence, and when he whomped my temple with his cocked pointer finger, and said he would've pulled the trigger had he had a gun, he must've forgotten I was his child.

When he came to my bedroom, awash with libertine urges, groped me, laid his body atop of mine, slipped his fingers inside my blouse and underwear, forced my hand between his legs saying, "*Play Daddy*," covered my mouth, respired raggedly, and thrust his damp and bulging nether region into my hip, he must've forgotten I was his daughter.

He kept my mouth closed—my legs opened.

Lights out.

I didn't squeal when he violated me that night. I needed to save my strength for later because I knew he'd do it for the rest of my life.

And that was life—a crossover between a boot camp and an infirmary. Routinely molested. Unfailingly surveilled.

Minutes turned into days, days into years, and torture every second in between. I slept with one eye open, sin after sin.

He was that intemperate and homicidal without a firearm. Imagine if he had one.

Whenever I heard his keys clacking and my door creaking, I knew they were the harbingers of horror—the boogeyman was home. I couldn't floss my teeth without him fondling me from behind and groaning his tumescent groin against my buttocks. He leered at me, like a sleepless vulture, and scooched his way beneath my blanket. I laid there lifeless as the crest of his head thudded against the headboard.

The monster was never under my bed—he was on it.

He was a tinderbox who detonated by the slightest affront. Any smudge of sedition would sanction semi-deadly force. With military training, his methods of attack left minimal to no markings that even gaping wounds were undetected to the naked eye. In this warpath, he was the commodore. Be subservient, or it's your funeral. He was a merciless beast with a thousand arms who suffocated me in his grip. When he banged his gavel, his word was law.

Demoralizing. Overbearing. Psychologically corrosive.

I knew the rug could be pulled from under me at a drop of a dime. My readiness to elude imminent threats didn't make me less scared, but it made me more adept in prophesizing when the dam would burst. It never got easier. Perpetually plagued by anticipation of impending dangers, I lived with a general inkling of dread and a heightened state of anxiety. Some nights, I was unfed, meaning any morsel could be my last. I didn't know when he'd whang a phone over my shin or publicly embarrass me again. If he gets distraught at the wheel again, would he ram us both into a flagpole or a Lock Raven abutment? Like he said he would?

Sometimes, I felt the whip before it even happened.

Vulnerability was a liability; a subset of weakness at home and elsewhere. Feelings detracted efficiency—only human feces and queasy hearts felt emotions—so, they were kept out of the equation. As a child, I didn't have a choice or an armor, so I've spent a lifetime enshrouded in one—a thick one. I'm a virtuoso of bogus smiles. No one's better at it.

My father measured people with metrics and honorifics. He held me to insatiable standards of etiquette and solidity—as you would with a cyborg. He waited at the finish line with rigid rules and strident expectations and adjudicated when I could earn my stripes. No kudos for second best or failure of any kind. No wiggle room, no second take. Excel or exit.

Rest, play, and progress were disregarded as low on his list. A huge house with turrets, prevalent recognitions, and top dollar outturn—that's a polished performer to him.

Subjected to corporal punishments whenever I scribbled an apostrophe as an oversight, I became incapable of slowing down. A do-gooder, a crowd-pleaser. I copped the degrees, the scholarships, and the medallions, but I was dwarfed by comparisons to the eminence of others when my curriculum vitae was less than stellar.

Unless I become a somebody, I was a nobody.

I took full blame for my undoing; my father took full credit for my success. Why? Because he had overblown feelings of self-importance and an irrational need for admiration. With bragging rights, he could admire himself in me.

This overview of success was so drilled in my head that I'd forgotten I had a heart. It was the Rorschach test and the teleprompter that framed the referendum by which I chose to interpret myself and the world. It was the tautological narrative under which all lies were subsumed.

Hope leaked out of me—poetry was my patch.

> *"How many times have people used a pen or paintbrush because they couldn't pull the trigger?"* - Virginia Woolf

Not having a pistol, I put pen to paper after discovering Shelly, Tennyson, Hardy, Byron, and Poe. Inspired and consoled by their timeless, seminal words, I unladed my despair into stories and journaled outside the lines and beyond the margins—an atypical pleasure for someone like me. My writings were prolix backlogs of heartbreaks, but they felt like parole from my penitentiary.

Words couldn't turn me back into that unsullied girl I once was, but with them, I thought I could be something.

I thought I could be a writer.

I loved literature so much, I disenrolled from biology and psych (*I had tepid inquisitiveness for the first and intense interest for the latter*) and switched my major to English—for less than a semester. My father thought my mutiny was an errant act to annihilate rather than a prospect to pursue.

Writers ate Ramen noodles, had meager earnings, lived in broom closets, and had nothing to tout but compendiums of florid prose and paperbacks. I was told it was a prosaic life, unless you're Tom Clancy or Danielle Steel. Even with my best entries, my words wouldn't be worth three of theirs.

After my father unleashed his riotous disapprobation on the campus lawn, I skedaddled to the Registrar and switched back—miserably so. My dream was not auspicious enough for his unsparing love, and such, this stamp of disapproval was ensued by a gazillion more. I felt vacant, but there were too many explosives to risk putting my passion in ink.

Stricken and stunned into silence by the same fear was my mother. She knew he violated me at night, again at sunrise, then attended church at noon—no remorse. She heard him evangelized his "*strict*" Catholic life on Sundays, but didn't observe it on any other day, and she knew the miasma of misery that upended my belief in a benevolent world, but it didn't matter. What he'd done to me was neither his first nor the most inbred. She thought our life and our family's life back home would be unaffordable if she left him, and that he'd intermit his support of them if she did. This was our debt to him, which we overpaid with servitude.

I saw my mother as a dolly, my father, a ticking bomb.

I disobeyed at times, and my insolence set off damaging techniques of *"discipline."* I learned not to goad the true enormity of my father's combustible temper. His fury was far in excess of my adolescent strength.

I was tight-lipped about the limousine life afforded to us by the very man I abhorred. It was as repugnant to undergo as it was to witness, and I'd *never* wish for anyone to gain this perspective. To the watching world, we had a charmed life, but we were showmen, and it was our sworn duties to hide the ugly, contaminated truth—as if it were a state secret. When not secluded at home, genuflecting, Mum and I were debutants in full regalia, punctilious about not letting the fissures show. This staged unity maximized our survival.

Inside the classroom, I couldn't write a sentence. Out of my cell, I was outlawed from saying a word.

This was the so-called life I was jinxed to live. Incessant emotional, physical, and mental torture. At age ten, I didn't think I'd live to see eleven. I had to freeze or *"fly away."*

Disassociation was—and still is—my coping mechanism for chronic traumas. A mental disorder; a disjuncture from reality. I'm involuntary extricated from my own body as I watch the world and myself transposed into an unreal glob, then I'm gone—no memories. Lumped that with purging, binging, insomnia, posttraumatic stress disorder, anxiety, mania, depression, dysmorphia, and an anorexic pendulum that had swung from scrawny to obesity, thin to wispy, to metabolic acidosis, and then back to emaciation, and you got yourself an outlier who never measured up—and in the breadth of her being—was never whole.

I wanted to dull pain.

I attempted the most ungrateful exit—more than once—but the Man upstairs deterred me from nuking myself. I know suicide wouldn't undo an era of torments, but no one could help me, and I could no longer face my fate. In some ways, I was already a corpse, pushed past the human allowance of agony—beyond the point of breaking. Against all odds, I had to either save myself or die trying.

On the run for relief and refuge, anything outweighed the landmines at home. I slept on friends' sofas, beanbags, and university futons with cardboards for a duvet, I washed up in public bathrooms, ate cafeteria leftovers, $0.99 burritos, and uneaten grub from my summer gig. Some ladies in the dorm allowed me to snooze on their bunk beds when their roommates weren't around, and when both mattresses were occupied, I slept on their desks.

> *"It is easier to build strong children than to repair broken men."* - Frederick Douglas

Innocence lost doesn't come with a refill, but shame will overtake you at every opportunity. Your sense of worth will diminish—if you had any left at all.

If a child survives something as horrific as abuse or abuse itself, how does she even move on unscathed? She doesn't. Abuse will have her call everything into question, trusting no one implicitly. On the flipside, bereft of unconditional love, she'll seek affection, security, love, and stability from anyone to fill her gaps. She could outstrip others in the workplace and try to counter her own defective design by embedding herself among the downcast and offering them hope, but she'd still be a vagabond—at war with herself.

I wasn't on speaking terms with my father, but recently, we've had talks—far and few in between. They have to be. Sordid and episodic memories of him combined with old, unconfident recordings of self-disgust and self-pity still get replayed. Here's my self-sabotaging, mental soundbite:

'I'm a nurse, but not a doctor. I'm petite, but not pretty. I'm thin, but not tall. I'm creative, but dorky. My boobs are ok, but my booty is saggy. I have a home, but not a mansion. I have a Master's, but not a doctorate."

Need I go on?

I was fed a steady diet of rejection. External validation was air to my lungs and rewards were nutrients to my bones, but I'd never felt full. Whenever I looked in the mirror, my parents' debauchery was staring back at me.

I can't remember when I stopped loving my parents. I can't recall when—if ever—I started loving myself.

IV – GO GREEN

"As I walked out the door toward the gate that would lead to my freedom, I knew if I didn't leave my bitterness and hatred behind, I'd still be in prison."
- Nelson Mandela

8. SPRING CLEANING

"If you hate a person, then you are defeated by them."
- Confucius

Undrgraduate classes at 08:00 seldom rousted me out of bed, but I scuttled to my psych courses with unquenchable curiosity by 07:45. All syllabi were scintillating: the id; the ego; Neo-Freudianism; archetypes; phobias; psychoanalysis; and theories of personality (*my fav*). The more insidious the etiology, the closer I leaned in. For the most part, I learned why people do what they do.

But there's one thing my formal education didn't teach me. I've lived throughout and despite all of its kind, yet it's still beyond my comprehension. It's beyond impudent, beyond brazen. It's wrong as wrong can be.

Abuse. Child abuse.

"Those who've been victimized by child sexual predators are frequently haunted by memories of these crimes well into their adulthood—often for the rest of their lives. They bear the burden of someone else's criminal behavior," said FBI Assistant Director Bill Sweeney.

The numbers are alarming: In the U.S., 1,840 children died of abuse and neglect in 2019; 1 in 4 girls and 1 in 13 boys are sexually abused; 1 in 20 children are physically abused yearly; child abuse is reported every 10 seconds; there are 42,000,000 sexual abuse survivors; and the cost of child abuse and neglect in 2015 was estimated at $428 billion.

For that of child sexual abuse, $9.3 billion—underreported.

How could you forgive the unforgivable?

I thought I'd be safe under the aegis of those I trusted, but I learned the insufferable lessons of abuse in their hands, and their irretrievable words and inexcusable actions left the hardest dent of hate. Outflanked by flashbacks, triggers, and explicit memories, I built an Alcatraz, cocooned myself in consternation, ruminated on revenge and an eye for an eye restitution, and waited for the vengeance fever to break. Embittered, I've lost connection with others. Baffled, I've lost connection with myself.

Emotionally compartmentalizing. Deflecting. Numbing.

For years, I was saddled with resentment—steeped in bare-knuckle anger. I dwelled on the wrongdoings of those who had long since atoned and disgorged my power into their hands—even to those of the deceased who had long found their peace. I waited for apologies that never came, unable to turn a new leaf. Nothing inured my heart and derailed my recovery more than the act of holding on to grudges.

Forgiveness is at the gist of Christian, Judaic, and Islamic teachings and a moral virtue in Buddhism. It sounds noble in theory. It's romanticized in songs, romcom, and movies. It's ubiquitously preached, but dismally practiced because to turn the other cheek is to put your big pants on.

I robbed myself of peace with so much wrath, Sheol wasn't hot enough for those I hated. I've stewed in both emotions long enough to know they're one and the same. They took turns mutating into viruses neither my body nor soul could expunge. As they metastasized into inoperable tumors, my heart stiffened—semidetached, opaque. I could extract the lessons and discard old pain or stay entangled. I could keep picking at maturated scabs or have hope supplant hate.

Horrendous as it all was, I chose forgiveness.

> *"The weak can never forgive. Forgiveness is the attribute of the strong."* - Mahatma Gandhi

Forgiveness was my antigen; my saving grace. It allayed thirty years of ghoulish emotions that hobbled over me—if not for the good of all, for my own healing. Letting go was of the uppermost importance in finding peace and coming to a better understanding of myself and those who maimed me. Unreeled, my opinions of both changed.

And I had a full docket to forgive.

I forgave the universe.

It's easier to look out a window than in a mirror, so I cursed

I cursed the cosmos for not curbing me from the rim of my insanity. I arraigned the world for turning away during my horror and grief. But how could I blame the universe for not seeing me when I've spent all my life under a bushel of protective devices? Too snooty to show pain; too gutless to dismantle the stories that had held me captive. I eschewed a truckload of unprocessed traumas, but immersed in ire and mistrust, it was implausible to circumnavigate them.

Without forgiveness, I handed hatred another feat.

It was not I against the draconian world as I once believed. This dichotomy pilfered me of gratitude and joy. Through forgiveness, I realized—time and time again—this world had blessed me with unstinting strength to spare under the most atrocious circumstances.

I forgave my mother.

I was angry at her for having me live with my father despite all the years of abuse that took place in plain sight and his incursions that put our lives in jeopardy. What my mother saw my father do to me was far more than spanking and scolding—they were lecherous and unlawful.

Befouled, I thought my pointless life was not just one she endangered, but one she condoned.

She could've told my father to sod off. She could've called the police, a priest, a social worker, a hotline. She could've taken us to a halfway house. She could've done a hundred other things, but didn't. She could've believed me when I told her explicitly about his improper touches, but didn't.

I'd only asked two people in my life to believe me, and one of them was my mother.

My mother dismissed my assertion of abuse from my father as a libidinous complex—Oedipus complex. I was told that the filthy things he did to me, I must've *"wanted them."* And should I so much concoct or tattle such untruth ever again, there'd be guys with a straitjacket to manhandle me from Sheppard Pratt—a psychiatric asylum in Baltimore. And with that admonition is how you muzzle an eleven-year-old child—a loose cannon—and retch her heart open.

My father was her brick and mortar—her rainmaker. She was nothing, if not his wife. In codependency, immobilized by a parochial mindset, her hope rose only to fall again with her flailing faith—like a seesaw. She was always ready to quit her marriage, but never had a pang of courage to leave. Too many excuses; too many quasi-egresses. Like a fugitive, for decades, she'd hunkered down in my house for days, weeks, sometimes months, but when he wheedled her that *"he's changed,"* yet again, she ran back to him and his web of infractions—every time.

For all of her life and most of mine, her indecision and fear crucified us to a life with him—a toss-up between fighting for my life and wanting to take it.

Mum couldn't find a life outside of my father. I don't think she knows one exists.

I'd watched her dissolved into a suburbanite doormat and a grinning sidepiece whom my father showboated on a short leash. The wrong in him, she promoted; the right thing to do for me, she overlooked. She was tacitly complicit with the devil incarnate in haggling my childhood for his game of Simon Says. She acted in concert with him in making my life reprehensibly imperfect. *¿Para qué?* A modicum of togetherness and marital grandstanding? When she wasn't

She spoke of him as if she were nominating him for father of the year. Other times, she was looking the other way or ululating into melodramatic bouts of syncope, having me fret over her rigor and take care of her afterward—making everything about her and leaving things unsolved.

How could a mother brainwash her daughter into believing *"If it wasn't for you, I would've left him a long time ago"*? It was her premise—one I believed—it was *my* fault. I was the reason my mother was in the doghouse, beholden to the grim reaper. I handcuffed both of us to a life of foreboding. I was the final arbiter of our fate.

She was the parent! I was a child! I had as much control over our situation as I had over the weather. Why didn't my safety take precedence over her own personal attrition?

I wasn't that jejune to not see how backward it all was.

I left home at twenty-one with less than $20 in hand. I lived in the dorm and worked in the lab. Mum chose to stay, so by then, her pretext was a crock. She was her own stricture.

I was riddled with inestimable anger towards my mother.

I've held her in such low regard that I've forgotten this was the woman who supported herself in high school and night classes doing mani-pedis, haircuts, and perms, punked her headmistress with her college roomies (*including a former Miss Philippines*), and chatty with co-alum Imelda Marcos about *Bayanihan* dancers and fine arts. The single mother who raised me for seven years while my ever unreachable playboy father cavorted with harlots, and she rode a tricycle *and* jeepney with me on weekdays so I could go to the best school in *Pilipinas*. The Florence Nightingale who nursed and mollified her husband and his erratic behaviors through cancer and chemo—undervalued and overworked. She was the only one who interjected between my father and me and quelled the firestorm brought on by my insubordination. The backbone of the Delos Reyes family and our bulwark against derisions and a century-old vendetta from the same bloodline—even more so after her brother's death.

My mum was the medic who painstakingly kept our home aseptic and changed my bandages when my three-year-old face, limbs, and torso got toasted with third-degree burns.

My father's ungoverned lust and manpower did not skip a generation. I wasn't his first victim—my mother was.

And still, she chose to give her unborn a chance to live. She chose to carry in her womb the marginalized fruit of the lascivious tree who wrested control over her and her body. She chose to keep her baby. She chose to keep me.

She'd lived under siege before I was even born and under his thumb every day after. Every move was picked apart, and there was little to nothing a prisoner could control. She *(and I)* tiptoed around him as to test my father's patience was to foment a tiger in a cage. One act of irreverence, one wrong curtsy, one wrong syllable—he'd go into apoplexy and upbraid her—like a watchdog and a warden. He told her she'd lived an undistinguished life—one with *"nothing to show for."* She thought she'd never amount to anything, just a window treatment who escorted him to ballrooms and jamborees. She had that image to upheld.

My mother quailed and comported in his world and became inactive in her own. Her self-esteem crumpled, along with her voice. I don't know if she had lost her will to dream or she thought she had no right to dream at all.

Either way, when a mother's undefended, no child is safe.

Mum and I were corralled under the same roof of terror and torment and survived the same cataclysmic conditions.

Skip ahead twenty years to when divorce snagged me into a dungeon and opened my eyes to the many vicissitudes of marriage. I sank deeper into the sulk—needing my mother even more—and no other confluences of events requited my anger towards my mother like her unabating presence. I was irresolute; she was mighty. Her incontrovertible love waded and salved me from the shards of divorce. My rock, cheerleader, chaperon, and best friend in every sense of the word—my lighthouse in an otherwise abysmal world. She helped me live another day.

If ever a doubt dangled around about her ability to protect her cub, she eliminated it.

She saved my life, and I understood hers in the process.

For the first time after not being on the best of terms, I saw my Mum through the prism of a woman and that of a wife. What I've endured in my marriage made me realize what she'd endured in hers. I pretended to love my husband; she pretended not to need hers. Her muffled pain spliced with my pain; her anguish intertwined with my anguish. With and through forgiveness, a junction called empathy heaved open, and slowly, our nuanced relationship began to heal.

Without judgment, I saw through her with compassion. I saw in her the good and sought to forgive the indefensible. We weren't the same people that we were before my father. After him, she did try to recapture her life, but keeping his child—me—the affirmation of his most unjustifiable act—made it more unlikely for her to recoup it. Mum said I'm *"the most precious thing"* to her, but does the boon of having a baby offset the despicable act that produced it? Mum participated in her own deterioration, blubbered for years in silence, and placed her husband's life ahead of her own. I didn't fall far from that tree.

Say what you will about my mother—call her a patsy or a puppet—but she's a woman of unquestionable strength.

Mum and I are closer now than we've ever been, bonded in our kindred brokenness and interminable trust. Forgiveness led us both to greater love and respect for each other. If we're in a pickle, we got this going for us. We're coming to terms with our pasts through an ongoing journey to being our own person and being whole.

If parents are fortresses at life's battlegrounds, consider my mother my citadel.

IN COLOR | JG GARCIA

"A mother's love for her child is like nothing else in the world."
- Agatha Christie

As for my father? It's a topic best forgotten.

I rebuffed him, cursed him, demonized him. I'd been on a rollercoaster ride to hell and back with him. I'd all but act out series of retributions (*all of which involved a shovel*) to decimate him as much as he had ruined me. He'd given plenty to our family—for that I'm grateful—yet he'd taken so much more. He's my father, my genetic makeup. Sired by him, I'm the devil's spawn. My unattainable desire for control, speed, accomplishment, and perfection stemmed from his officious voice that rung from my prepubescent years into the early aught. From the orifices of my body to the pit of my soul, there's no part of me he had not infected beyond ablution.

My affairs—including marriage—were all dysfunctional, but I put up with them because, at least, the best thing about those guys was that they were not my father. I'd talk your ear off about what a nimrod he was, but don't you dare call my man "*Ike*" and me "*Tina*"! (*Now, excuse me as I hide my bruises*). Whether it's parenting, political, or personal, when all your hatred is aimed at one man, it makes other predators look like the Pope.

Stories of my father aren't my favorite to retell. He stood for everything satanic. Because of him, I know everything there is to know about pain and misery, and for payback, I wanted him to suffer as I knew nothing about forgiveness.

How could I grant clemency to this albatross, this human chode who'd offended all canons of purity?

Addled by astronomical anger, I couldn't see that in thirty years of hating my father, I was hating myself.

My beleaguered, pill-popping life was no fluke. Hatred of that size—or any size for that matter—is a headlock of emotions that achieve nothing of value. I was soaked in a sewage of acrimony, marinated in shame, without upward movement. I couldn't safeguard my sanity—not when the mental rumpus wouldn't stop. Old grazes festered with a pungent smell billowing over me like an overcast. Frazzled with incalculable fear, I trusted no one—not even myself.

I had a bazillion reasons to harbor hate towards my father, but when it came to forgiving him, I had but one: to find peace. Through forgiveness, in conjunction with unsettling trips to my therapist, I deconstructed traumas that were too graphic and residuals too raw, and unfastened myself from the blackmails, gaslighting, and proselytizing.

I buried the hatchet by necessity and by choice.

Are we so riven, we're unbridgeable? Will he ever grow a conscious, and cough up apologies to everyone he'd hurt? It's anyone's guess. But the answers are inapplicable to my life now because he's not much in it. I can't overexert my forbearance—I have little of it left for him. He knows this; he'd long stopped ingratiating himself to me with any form of concord.

Forgiving my father was immeasurably grinding.

And while I was at it, I forgave myself.

I've done a caboodle of dastardly deeds at the expense of many: execrable shit to my Rolodex of romances; uncalled for quips to friends; ungodly acts to kins; brotherhood I've breached; those I disrespected; and relationships I jilted and left in tatters without a minute's thought.

And the sins I've committed against myself…

For the things I should've said, but didn't, and the loops I didn't close, I mouthed, *"I'm sorry, I'm sorry, I'm sorry,"* out into the ether, hoping God's heralds would funnel my tearful words to the ears of those hearts I've assailed. The brunt of compunction weighed heavily in my conscious, but retrograding to my past transgressions—face to face—would cause damages that'd be far greater than the truce.

The less I said, the better.

An upfront apology isn't always the best course of action to expiate one's guilt. Whether or not they'd exculpate me, it was my choice to repent—theirs was to forgive.

Do you need to forgive yourself? How about those you may have scalded? Can you chug down that acrid ampoule of pride, apologize without excuses, and ask for forgiveness?

Forgiveness is a choice and a maze. In your time, when you're ready and willing, move through the pain, isolation, and betrayal. When you fully let go, you can fully receive. Forgiveness moves the needle from pandemonium to peace. Think of it as an exterminator who scours your soul from emotional vermin and mental mildews. It renews the soul with compassion, the mind, with awareness. It's a vehicle that moves you forward with less resistance. It's known to improve cardiovascular health and lower stress and anxiety.

I'm not insinuating it's a cinch to vindicate, but if you're an apostate of forgiveness, ask yourself if execrating through life with hatred, anger, and guilt sounds like a cakewalk?

Forgiveness has different meanings to different people, none of which to be assumed as a mechanical reconciliation or an exoneration of all malcontents. For some, it's not an initiative for another round of dodgy behaviors, a green light to reconnect, or a revolving gate for repeat offenders. Culpability doesn't guarantee a reprieve. An olive branch isn't a clearance for the velvet rope to go down. Reentry can still be debarred.

What about the axiom, *"Forgive and forget"*?

"Forgivers are not weaklings. They stand in the truth that they have been treated with injustice and they respond with a softened heart, with the paradox that they themselves become emotionally healed," said Robert Enright, Ph.D. of *Psychology Today*.

Forgivers don't have to do anything other than forgive.

And for others, forgiveness is inconceivable no matter how much your contrite heart grovels.

And if our nation can call the Taliban our new *"frenemy," "diplomatic,"* and *"businesslike,"* and laud a British Royal, who once dressed up as a Nazi, and then put him on the cover of *TIME* magazine, maybe we can take a break from the demerits and forgive others so they could, at least, host *The Bachelors* or *Jeopardy!*.

Waiting for apologies? They may never come. You can't coerce people to own up to their blunders any more than you can force anyone to remit you. Forgiveness isn't for them; it's for you. It's an internal gift you give yourself.

Are you perforating yourself with a cilice of guilt? Is your indignation humongous enough to smother a stadium? Life is so dear and forgiveness so unbounding to be basted with hate. Hate conflated with anger or guilt is not an equalizer of injustice, but a despoiler of judgment, healing, hope, and foresight. Let them go, and make peace with your past.

As for the rest of the riff-raff on my forgiveness docket? It's underway.

9. RULES OF DISENGAGEMENT

"To injure an opponent is to injure yourself. To control aggression without conflicting injury is the Art of Peace."
- O Sensei Morihei Ueshiba

Some folks can take a ribbing and not lose their cool. When heckled during a dialectic exchange of theses, they stay unflappable, and when the challenger turns archrival, they put their advisability to good use. They can deescalate a debate when it crescendos from genial into a full-frontal contention by walking away in *hāmau* (*silence*), with dignities intact, pride unruffled, and without a nagging need to prove their point.

Such class. Such grace. Such self-control.

Not so with me.

No, Sir. I was never one to lower my sword. I'm not proud of it, so I say this with a tinge of mortification.

It didn't take much to strafe my easily contused ego into red-zone defensiveness: any and all contortions of the truth; untrue imputations; glib commentaries; people not calling back within thirty seconds of me leaving them a voicemail. Every ignoramus, lie, snark, and quibble got under my skin. If you connived against me or forayed my character with or without a disjointed argument, you're a dirtbag, and must be summarily eviscerated. I'd go into overdrive, wrestling drama with drama, malarkey with malarkey

Progressively crabby, I was ready to cut a bitch.

I was either a dormant volcano, erupting with molten lava, or a well-oiled machine, cannonading from all cylinders like Rambo with a belt-fed M60-E3 gun—depending on how caffeinated I was.

So, when a ghost from my past (*the bane of my existence*) recruited his intermediaries into a multifront scrimmage against me, I girded myself for a Defcon 5 rematch. These unscrupulous doofuses had maligned me in copious ways that I turned to Jesus to not retaliate and go to jail. Mounds of lies overlapped as friction rocketed among this ratpack.

Playing defense, I was so gung-ho to set the record straight, cudgel the truth out of them, and clear my name.

Did you think I was going to crouch? Hell no! I was no pushover, no wimp. I would not be outgunned! I would not be pilloried! This clash called for a two-prong onslaught. React not recede!

I had a rousing speech cobbled with facts and snapshots. I rehearsed it in my head in high definition and slow motion. What if Deputy Dawg and his puny minded, sociopathic lieutenants had a stern offense? How do I reload? Refuel?

In case of an unforeseeable shakedown, I had to enlist my own sparring partner to help me effectuate a recrimination. A politic counterattack. Such was my ironclad stratagem.

I called my friend Martha.

"What do I say if he says this…? Or she says that…?"

I thought she'd be my reinforcement, but she smacked me back to my senses and stopped me in my tracks.

"You don't have to engage," she said.

Mind blown. I—Don't—Have—To—Engage. WTF? Was that a euphemism for *"Shut your pie hole"*? JG befuddled.

After weeks of crosstalk and months of contemplation, I realized Martha had let me in on one of the esoteric secrets of adulthood: regulating one's emotions. It was about time someone called me out on my immaturity and inability to guard my own.

As the spectacular friend that she is, Martha's ceasefire had me reflect and reevaluate how I handle—or mishandle—hostility. She knew it was best for me to step away—that scum and his minions had nothing to say but pejoratives. She didn't enable me to go down that rabbit hole with more ammunition. By not refereeing that catfight, she made me realize silence has been a forgotten form of self-respect.

Haplessly, I've spent most of my surly life overreacting and lashing out to warring forces. My ego took the lead, and emotions invariably followed. The idea of capitulating was uneasy and outlandish. Anger was my default response. I'd be so engrossed in quick-fire emotions, spouting every barb I had in my confrontational toolbox, that the conversations often stopped being a scout for the truth and became a carnival of Chewbaccas. When pleasantries overheated into intemperate gabbing, cuckoo's nest JG came out with gears turning, guns blazing. My inner bitch on a broom would be braying, *"Bring it on!"* If I were pecking out my words, I'd be yammering them in all caps, bold, and italic. Nothing was conciliated; I only made matters unnecessarily volatile.

I wore antagonism like a crown.

I fed the beast, and so it lived.

And after a fallout, I'd walk into a cognitive mousetrap and rephrase every bushwa said in the disagreement in a mental monologue—only to lose the imaginary brawl with myself.

Are we instinctively virtuous in our reasoning? Maybe. We all have our neurosis, and mine had me saying sardonic things that I couldn't unsay. I've infuriated a few and hurt a lot more. Too bumptious to flinch from lambasting others, I severed those ties, and they're now irreparable.

My postwar backfire was tamped with regrets: if I hadn't been Godzilla, I could've put a lid on it; if I hadn't sweated the small stuff, I could've returned to my breath; if I had taken a paralytic or two—or three—and swerve away from disputations, maybe I could've made amends.

If we disengage before a quarrel reaches its tipping point, and let silence slay the dragon, we can save relationships from further annihilation—and possibly ourselves.

Others may draw first blood, but you don't have to have the last word or win every argument or controvert every topic at length until you slug it out. Most things are answerable to time, if it's closure you want. Every action doesn't need an equal—or in my case—a gratuitous amount of reaction. Most dissensions desist if deprived of oxygen.

Take the verbal overhauling we now see on television. This climate is shrilling with rabid self-expression. Every zealot has something to say! It's an uprising during which people are bludgeoned for sentiments they say and don't say! Prochoice. Pro-life. Pronoun. Voting regulations. Elections. Deportations. Equity. Equality. Gender fluidity. Amnesty. Intersectionality. Fracking. Global warning. McCarthyism. Marxism. Socialism. Communism. Capitalism. Feminism. There's a mouthpiece for that.

If you can neither pronounce nor define these terms without Wikipedia, you have no business belaboring them.

"There's no freedom of speech if only one side is allowed to speak." - U.S. Representative Jim Jordan

But if you and/or your cabal have to use gas, nun chucks, industrial grade fireworks, Molotov cocktails, blowtorches, chemical irritants, canisters, crowbars, kerosene, machetes, pipes, Uzis, C4s, and/or 2x4s to underscore your words, maybe you shouldn't speak. If you and/or your goons have to belch up epithets, profanities, and incendiary rants and outbursts because you have the emotional maturity of a two-year-old, put a sock in it.

If you and/or lemmings can't listen to anyone on the other side of your ideological sector that you'd throttle, kneecap, or spritz them with saliva, demilitarize yourselves before you turn into a concretum of arsonists in a calaboose.

If midgame, you'll redefine words or pull them out of your rectum because you cannot win a tournament of thoughts with facts, logic, or erudite thinking, then shush it Webster.

If you're going to make a declaration by creating a mob of marauders, ravaging what others had built, running amok in freeways, and decapitating effigies as living indictments of lawlessness and illegalities, please evacuate.

To the thugs turned theologians, haranguing us to have a utopian future while you still live in the past with revulsion, brindle yourselves before you give yourselves an aneurysm. To the quacks, indoctrinating us to your worldviews, zip it. You're not an intellectual; you're a philistine who hasn't seen the world. To all you hobbits, sputtering flubdubs that don't jibe with scientific truth, but with the media mandate, you either have a flatulent mouth, a flatulent brain, or both. I won't truncate the anatomies here. To those pontificating about abolishing our country's maladies, you can start by not mongering its citizens.

To all virtue signaling juntas, politicizing pseudo-moralistic tenets on global soapboxes to sound like sociology savants on TikTok and Twitter, spare me your Orwellian overload and anti-Semitic jargon.

I'm a vegan—I know a word salad when I hear one.

For the street Spartacus taking umbrage at innocuous topics that nobody asked you to justify in the first place or don't directly affect your life, your unsolicited two cents could use a Ritalin. You're discoursing your opinions and airing your grievances in poor taste, like a sniveling baby in need of a diaper change. You're bristling with denotation, but unfilled of intellect: no fact-based rationale; no reputable data; no objective analysis. Blustering divergent theories gleaned from some bozo's bulletin doesn't train your mind.

Jumbled emotions muddle your faculty, and fuming away sophistries doesn't modulate your mood. They don't make you riotous, portentous, or philosophical. If anything—and I'm saying this with love—it makes you look like you've just undergone a lobotomy—or in need of one.

Before calling a doctrine *"bonkers,"* be quiet until you read the darn thing.

And before you flog me with expletives or have an orgy of pyromania if I like *"Macarena"* over *"YMCA"* or acoustic over acapella, and before you go berserk if my preference doesn't pander to yours, *De gustibus non est disputandum* (*in matters of taste, there can be no disputes*).

When I'm amped to speak, to judge, I reverse and rethink.

I've neither held a loaded gun nor had the decision to go home to my family or put a bullet in someone scrambled in a nanosecond, but should I lecture those who have been in the line of fire about safety and humanity because I've seen "*Indiana Jones*"? Or criticize a pregnant woman (*or is it "birthing person" now?*) for having an epidural because I myself don't take a Midol when I menstruate?

Not really the same thing, huh? Better to disengage.

> "*No man should judge unless he asks himself in absolute honesty whether in a similar situation he might not have done the same.*" - Dr. Victor Frankl
> (*from the greatest memoir I've read*)

You can stampede and belittle others with a steamroller and high-voltage feelings when they don't play fair or you can purge yourself of pride, and stand down. The world doesn't always revolve around you. If that's too unclear, allow me.

Whenever someone cut me in line, I was no lightweight. "*Helloooooooooooo! Do you not see me? Do you not know who I am? I'm JG! I'm a frontliner!*"

Take your Trazadone, tigress! Maybe I was holding up the line. Maybe it wasn't because I'm Asian or a woman or I'm an Asian woman. Maybe nobody gives a f*ck if my name is prepended to an R.N. or an M.D or L, M, N, O, P. And maybe, just maybe, they—just—did—not—see—me.

What do you want? Diplomacy or division? Relationships or rivalries? Disrepute or decorum?

If the mercury is boiling with the din of ruffians, if dullards prattle hogwash from the artilleries of their tiny minds, if gangbangers turbocharge at you, and if your tolerance isn't well received, walk away. Before surrogates of Mussolini, Stalin, Mao, Pol Pot, and Hitler put you in a cervical collar and/or a casket for wearing a red hat that they'll misread as Swastika, walk away. God forfend they overhear you say you're a patriot! Shrug them off, and end the to-and-fro on your terms. Don't deign to their level. Regain your power and composure. Knowing the value of your voice is sexy and mature, and so is learning that of your silence.

A true and dispassionate warrior adapts to his enemies with voluntary control.

If I were to rectify every mendacious crap, every Pinocchio claim, debunk every baseless misrepresentation, and rebut every fable and erroneous blame chided at me, I'd have a second full-time job—unpaid.

Nothing says, *"I'm done with you,"* like blaring silence.

Plus, give karma some room to strike (*it sure did with me*).

According to a study by the University of Michigan, a dash of arguing is beneficial to your health. But no wisecracks or verbal roasting!

Marriage therapist Marissa Nelson said, *"Argument should never be a character assassination, or bring someone's integrity into question."*

Even in opposition, there's leeway to calmly refrain from invectives, and respect each other. Silence begets distance, distance begets clarity, and clarity can create a longing for unfeigned reconnection. But you've got to let the flame go out without going jugular. If someone agrees with you, it doesn't automatically mean you're right. If they disagree with you, it doesn't automatically mean they're wrong.

"The best answer to anger is silence."
- Marcus Aurelius

Silence is a lost art—let's revive it. It takes awareness and an imperturbable mind. It is as facile as it is taxing. It isn't for the minor league. It's too delicate a dance for weenies to learn.

It took forty years to implant this lesson in my pigheaded skull, but I've had a direct departure from my defunct, Jerry Springer takedown. Every so often, jackasses bait me—the irascible me—and I do not disappoint. *Obrigada*, Martha! When I'm roiling with firepower, her equanimity is like a tranquilizing hybrid of Oolong tea and Tibetan chants.

Martha also reminded me of that time I opted to stay silent.

It was 2012. I've been undefeated in Scrabble since 1986. After thirteen rounds, (*ex-hubby*) Carlos was still on a quest to topple my twenty-six-year winning streak. On the next one, cross-eyed and overtired, I carelessly left the bottom right of the board game open, and Carlos pipped me with a Double Word Score *and* a Triple Word Score with letters: Q-U-I-T-E. He swanked, *"Ha! I beat you with QUIET!"*

I could've gone ballistic, but I chose not to say a word.

"Better to remain silent and be thought of a fool than to speak out and remove all doubt."
- Abraham Lincoln

10. IT'S A RAP

"That which does not kill us makes us stronger."
- Friedrich Nietzsche

The 2002 Academy Award for Best Original Song was *"Lose Yourself"* from the blockbuster sensation *8 Mile,* starring Eminem as Jimmy *"B-Rabbit."* In the movie, he and another phenom Clarence *"Papa Doc"* lobbed lyrical slanders at each other and showcased their vocal gymnastics with rhythm and rhyme. Pertinacious all the way to the last round, B-Rabbit, *"proudly"* freestyled comprehensive verses of his *"trailer white trash"* life and Doc's *"private school"* upbringing (*nullifying Doc's hood credibility*). Throwing the mic to Doc, he challenged him: *"tell these people something they don't know about me."*

Nothing more to say. Nothing more to blab.

Mortified and speechless in front of a feisty audience, Papa Doc kowtowed to B-Rabbit's preemptive victory.

Ok, who's next?

Who wants to satirize their bungles and flack their failures and inadequacies at the risk of ridicule and against the vast hypocrisy of online perfection? Who am I kidding? We'd rather toot our own horns. Toot! Toot!

Paul Krugman of the *New York Times* wrote, as a nation, we're suffering from an *"epidemic of infallibility."*

If you fear failure and mistakes, like most, join the club. I used to tremble at the thought of failure. I've fallen flat on my face more than I could quantify, but I was too uppity to shine the spotlight on my own vices; I was incorrigible. By pretending my infirmities weren't real in fear of flack and mockery, I denied my imperfections and weaseled my way out of them. I rendered myself pompous and impermeable. These contrivances were doubly nifty during job interviews (*so I could give myself a rave*) and at the start of a budding romance (*so I wouldn't appear so unattractive*), but only momentary—they hurt me in the long run.

Failure is right up my wheelhouse. Over time, my scanty misdoings added up into colossal disasters, baying for me to own them. In doing so, a pattern coalesced: I'd been on a carousel of the same old coverups, but on different days and different places; different lies with different guys.

I stopped lying to myself and, once again, turned inward. I asked myself caustic questions that penetrated my baloney bubble: Why does vulnerability makes me want to vomit? Why was I so averse to failure? Whose reproach left me believing my flaws defined my character? How long could I hide my glumness in the basement before others see it?

From there, it's been a circuitous journey to awareness of how I got buffeted to where I was.

Once I vacated my defensive stance, I realized none of us is exempted from the responsibility of asking these questions to explore what it means to be human, and to be human is to be fallible—as trite as that may sound.

If repurposed for personal growth, failures aren't fruitless.

"You are much better off admitting that something is wrong and addressing it in as authentic and transparent way possible," said Charlene Li of *Harvard Business Review*.

For starters, I cringed at the thought of being wrong. Why?

Who the hell knew? I didn't look for answers I didn't want to find! I've overdosed on my own supply of lame excuses that my knee-jerk reaction was to avoid blame or assign it where it didn't belong. It drove a wedge between me and loved ones, and stymied me from seeing my fingerprints on my mistakes and unhappiness.

I brood over these relationships, knowing had I not been so slick at self-justification, I could've conserved them.

Then there's failing and how self-censorious I was at it. One infinitesimal slip-up and I tamped myself down with a mallet and burrowed away at past misdemeanors. I'll share my dietary regimen to illustrate this point,.

To kickoff 2020, I went from being a vegetarian to a vegan. A novice, I inadvertently purchased something with milk and egg *"derivatives."* But I judiciously read the label!

"I'm so stupid! A month as a vegan and I already failed! This is why I'm fat! On Lipitor! I cheated with chicken when I was a vegetarian; ow I'm eating eggs! My diet is down the toilet! I can't do this! I fail at everything!"

That's an example of one of my mild self-talks—and it was only pastries, not a college denial letter or anything.

PETA didn't pelt me with rotten tofu. There wasn't a vegan police detaining my ass. Drs. Colin Campbell and Caldwell Esselstyn, Jr. didn't deem me excommunicated from the plant-based, whole-food brethren. It was me, internalizing mishaps the wrong way. The unhealthy way.

"Unless you learn to respond to failures in psychologically adaptive ways, they will paralyze you, demotivate you, and limit your likelihood of success going forward," said Guy

Winch, Ph.D. of *Psychology Today*. Failures distort your perceptions of your goals and abilities *"by making you feel less up to the task. Once you fail, you are likely to assess your skills, intelligence, and capabilities incorrectly and see them as significantly weaker than they actually are,"* per Dr. Winch.

The doctor's right. Every failure curtailed my abilities and lengthened the distance between me and my aspirations. This far-reaching pervasiveness torpedoed my self-esteem and how I viewed the world—and myself. Life felt fallow. Then I took a gander at failures from a new paradigm and learned one unarguable fact: it's omnipresent.

Failure is rancid, but it makes success taste sweeter.

When our failures are unsaid, we forswear all eventuality to the whim of fate—leaving us powerless. But failures can embattle us psychologically to overcome obstacles and repair what we don't t want to repeat. Stop purporting that all is hunky-dory when your health, your relationships, or your career is proof that the converse is true. When we unbind ourselves from the reluctance to acknowledge our failures, we stop creating excuses for them. Blind spots come into focus. We self-correct, not self-destruct.

We don't receive wisdom by basking in the alight gleam of self-righteousness—believe me, I've tried. It's a virtue we acquire by learning from imperfections. There's humility in admitting our fragility, and in humbleness, we can interpret errors as mellow prompts that we all fail, but we're not failures. We're malleable humans trying to come to terms with our frailties, without devaluing our meaningful mess.

It's a step closer to seeing the beauty of our broken parts.

"Failure is simply the opportunity to begin again, this time more intelligently." - Industrialist magnate Henry Ford

Failure befalls us all, but with a function! Why not lean into the lessons of your invidious past, and come out wiser on the other end? Recompose and outdo yourself.

I don't know about you, but I no longer want the behemoth burden of perfection. The judgment calls I've made in my twenties were bad, thirties were gaumless (*as most of them turned out*), in my forties, they were less specious. But my best stories are the offshoot of my dumbest decisions—my masterclasses. And I'm not done with my idiocies! There's still an armful of unwise moves to be made.

Acknowledging our downfalls makes us better humans and for some—not all—incorruptible leaders.

"People don't expect perfection from their leaders… when leaders are honest about their shortfalls and can learn from their mistake, they earn respect and along the way create an environment of transparency," said Glenn Llopis of *Forbes*.

"Victory has a hundred fathers, but defeat is an orphan."
- John F. Kennedy

In that speech, Kennedy took the heat for Cuba and the Bay of Pigs Invasion. Camelot owned what he'd inherited from Eisenhower *and* took accountability for his failed foreign policies and militaristic rout (*bad, but not the worst*). This President didn't call his failure an *"extraordinary success."*

Richard Nixon confessed to misleading his country. Ronald Reagan apologized for the actionable use of proceeds that occurred under his watch. Bill Clinton—yes, there was the finger-wagging repudiation of adultery (*didn't think I'd see that coming?*), but he did admit his lewd involvement with his intern thereupon (*And why was he lecturing another President about misbehaving in the Oval Office?*).

Barack Obama took office in 2009, and 66% of Americans said race relations were good then. By 2015, 61% said they were bad. In Obama's last State of the Union address, he stated, *"It's one of few regrets of my presidency... the suspicion between the parties has gotten worse instead of better."* He later reiterated, *"The politics had become more rancorous during my presidency and more polarized than when I came in."* His words, not mine.

The Roman Catholic Church denounced Galileo for his hypothesis that the Earth wasn't the center of the universe. The physicist then recanted his discoveries—that or char at the stake. He was apprehended for nearly a decade, but over three-hundred years later, Pope John Paul II said the Church erred and admitted Galileo was right.

Failure spares no one—not commoners, vicars, or veritable men of Pennsylvania Avenue, but acceptance of dereliction and failings gains deference, admiration, and trust.

I'd be remiss if I don't broach vulnerability.

It was my most reviled word in the English language; the *"the 'V' word"* as I called it. It was too frightening to my iceberg interior, so don't say it in my presence! I thought it was a character defect, but now, I'm humming a different tune. Showing vulnerability—not the way these histrionic, little sissies do—doesn't emit weakness. It fosters a culture of compassion and synergy, and with emotional safety nets, others feel invited to reciprocate.

At times, part of professing your gaffes is apologizing.

I thought an apology was an admission of guilt, and saying *"I'm sorry"* made me choke. I've said, *"I'm sorry if,"* or *"I'm sorry you feel that way."* That's the most ineffective, unapologetic, and insensitive apology! It's not a mea culpa! It's not even a perfunctory outreach! I've mistreated people and patently failed to value those relationships enough to swallow my pride and come clean.

If your apology is stilted with insincerities—or excuses—don't even bother giving one. Fessing up isn't about who's right, but what's right.

If you cannot recognize your failures and missteps, you're susceptible to those who can. If you've wronged or failed, others may have already noticed, but if you'd rather not highlight your foibles, your nonbelievers won't hesitate to point them out for you. Ever heard of *"haters"*? They'd want nothing more than to trash talk you, make you look and feel left out and less than, and capitalize on the skeletons in your closet. Good luck repressing them from what they already know.

Why hand over your control? Take back your power.

If you're B-Rabbit, faced against your most nefarious hater, what would you say? My lines may not hit a dulcet note, but I'd lay my fifty-two cards on the table. Here we go:

> *"You see what I want you to see.*
>
> *No one knows the real me.*
>
> *Not even you, who took my all.*
>
> *I'm still here. Standing tall.*

Tell your lies, gossips, and hate

to those morons you can manipulate.

You think you know what I'm about?

I'm a wounded warrior.

Go and try to figure me out."

Mic drop

V – TICKLE PINK

"I'm not afraid of storms, for I'm learning how to sail my ship."
- Louisa May Alcott

11. BABY TALK

"No one can make you feel inferior without your consent."
- Eleanor Roosevelt

I know a cadre of nurses, and I don't share my withered dreams with them, but after a few sidebar natters, I felt a kinship with SyRina. Outside our vocation, we have a similitude of interests. This brunette goddess towers over me at 5'9, is married to a fireman, and has four adorable *keikis (children)*. SyRina respects the metaphysical without leaving logic behind. As a doting fur mum herself to Jax, her Golden Retriever, Syrina gets why I have a slew of my own dog's photos on my phone—all 4,000 of them.

On the topic of motherhood, I shared with SyRina that I did once dream of having my own little rascals—one for every baseball position. I pictured them rising to their alarm with punctuality, eating their buckwheat pancakes, chickpea and spinach omelets, and three servings of organic fruits. Then they'd quietly get in the car, we'd listen to Joel Osteen, and head to the beach after they'd said *"Please"* and *"Thank You"* to the Starbucks barista. For supper, my munchkins would eat their spaghetti and vegan meatballs with faultless table manners. Not a speck of sauce on their attires or on my beige, bateau neckline, Stella McCartney sheath dress. I'd swaddle my elves with their onesies and read to them *"Jack and the Beanstalk."* Hubby does the dishes and we'd all get eight hours of shuteye, including our Bulldog, Shih Tzu, Chowchow, Bichon, Lab, and Husky.

"Yeeeeeeah, JG. I don't live in that world," SyRina said.

Who the heck does? We sure had a good giggle!

In my Candy Land spaceship, a unicorn would also sing my goslings to sleep with fairy dust. SyRina's tales of child-rearing resemble reality, but she didn't sneer at my wishful concept of family—I appreciated that.

Days later, a semi-stranger woman inquired if I had kids. I said, " *I'm childless,*" She said, *"Is something wrong? A lot of women your age go in vitro."*

"Wrong"?

I don't have a gynecological condition. I made a choice.

"The vast majority of American women have children. Yet fewer women are deciding to become mothers: The fertility rate is at a record low," according to Claire Cain Miller of The New York Times.

Between 2014 and 2017, the CDC showed a precipitous drop in fertility rate—a groundbreaking low in over thirty years—and it ticked down by 1% from 2018 to 2019.

That woman's question was posited on a denigrating notion that my barren uterus was medically incompetent to bear fruit. Come on now, Sistah! We already greet ourselves with self-derogating women-to-women verbiage during our carb-free, gluten-free, fat-free luncheon with phrases like, *"Hello, I gained five pounds... I'm fat... I look like an orca... I'm bloated."* But my ovaries needing a reboot? Can we not go there?

Wahine (women) qualify for Army Ranger school, lead combatant directives, fly F-35 aircraft and UH-60 Black Hawk helicopters, coach in the NFL and basketball, and complete NASA's spacewalk, but if they don't give birth, is something is *"wrong"* with them?

What's with the relic mindset?

As a woman, I've been pigeonholed by gender bigotry and stereotypes into quadrants of predetermined timelines. As a Filipino, Asian woman, this triad comes with a timeline as well—a directory of prescribed roles and expectations. In the past years, I've felt the world was far less welcoming and supportive to women like me who veered off course and incised unconventional paths of our own choosing.

Certain breeds of comments imply that we, the unmarried, the divorced, the childfree, are disdained by high society or impertinent to principles and institutions or the black sheep of the family—or all of the above. Why? Because we've unsubscribed from prohibitive female roles and antiquated belief systems.

I know it's imperative to enshrine customs and rituals; I just don't let them have power over me. Can following my heart be an interface between the two?

Despite the dishonor that's traditionally tough to erase from the realms of divorce, I'm not radioactive—and you can't catch *Divorcetococcus pneumoniae* by shaking my hand. You cannot demote me with a marked-down sticker, like a half-off canned good. Nothing is wrong with my content; my inside is unblemished, my nub, undefiled. Same goes for my ilk. The divorcees I know are badass avatars of chutzpah, soulful beauty, and profundity.

Let's talk conceiving. What I think is interesting, and still perhaps unexplainable, is what does society think makes a woman's life vivacious? Is it what she lends to meritocracy from her head? Or shares from her heart? Or is it what she expels from her vagina? Does her life lack meaning from not procreating? Is a baby the barometer of her conformism or caste?

I was neurologically hardwired to marry and have children since my early years, and when—not if—I do, I'd be happy and no longer be astern of my wedded peers. I'd then earn the approbation to sit on the adult table. That was the pitch.

Per Noam Shpancer, Ph.D. of *Psychology Today,* we view parenting as a marker and *"an essential part of achieving fulfillment, happiness, and meaning in life."*

Once upon a time, I wanted the white picket fences, the sunporch, prams with cooing triplets, lollipops and Legos, ponies and pigtails, the onerous responsibilities of being a mummy—the whole shebang. Besides dogs, pandas, and koalas, nothing (*I mean nothing*) snuggles my heart like the sight of a father toting his child and holding his/her pudgy fingers during his/her first step, toddler martial arts, Fisher-Price stepstool and potty, bath splashes, bedtime stories, and mid-morning naps with slobbers on his chest.

I'm cognizant of the benefits of an equivalently committed partner. I've searched for the luxuries of having a husband and being a dual-career couple. I couldn't be unprepared—not in creating a life. It's close to $250,000 to defray the cost of raising a child *(excluding college)*, so I crunched economic metrics such as his career and financial footing. He didn't have to surpass my earnings, but not insolvent at the same time. His family values must be intransigent, our interests and life stages must align, and his emotional age, principles, and future trajectory must be suitable with mine.

I wanted to marry a man, and raise our children—I did *not* want to raise both.

There were honorable aspirants, but when it was time to show and tell, not one passed the acid test. No man rose to the challenge—neither did I. Our personalities flattered each other, but collided when things got cumbrous. We weren't the worse couple, but close to the bottom. What I had with them was an incubator of irreconcilable mayhem.

With awareness, I realized and accepted we're in different places. Our coordinates would never converge. I chose not to play Russian Roulette with me and my unfit options, and hope for the best. I couldn't gamble on that front. Acutely aware of the degree of difficulty of having a family, I chose not to throw their future up in the air, and see where the pieces would land. The only thing left to do was to let go.

Enough about them. I've limped and wobbled through the emotional labor of being in and out of relationships. I did not want to try my luck with that of pregnancy. Even if the embryo would be viable, I was far from viability.

"The percentage of single parents is higher in the U.S. than in other developed countries," said Dr. Shpancer.

In America, there are over 17,000,000 fatherless kids under the age of eighteen (*one in four*). They're 5x more likely to commit suicide, 14x more to become sexually aggressive, 20x more to have behavioral disorders, and 32x more to run away than kids with fathers at home. Nearly 45% of single-mother households live below the poverty line. It's dire—the literature on the effects of unstable, unsafe homes on behavioral issues, mental illness, and academic deficits.

With the shape I was in, mixed with my paternal candidates rap sheet, my progenies and I would've been on the express train to these distressing statistics.

I wanted my little geese to have the best family structure, and the best of their mum and dad—not what's left of them.

While I oscillated back and forth on being a mum, up to my mid-thirties, I watched my female friends, families, and their *keikis* to know one situation in comparison to another. These women have children for all kinds of reasons. Some make motherhood look unchallenging. To some, in tandem with their spouses' generous salaries, money's no object. Elite schools. Nannies. Chauffeurs. Villas. Glitzy holiday cards. Some feel there's no disconnection between them and their spouses, and they've forfeited their femininity and freedom by being stream-rolled into having kiddies. Some are falling off the financial cliff.

And others are floundering to supply the bare minimum.

And with very little sleep, some are disconsolate with low-grade resentfulness for their newborns.

To SyRina, parenting and survival mode look like this:

"I see moms making cute bento lunches with funny faces for sandwiches, sewing cute unique outfits… I see kids overly groomed, wearing outfits and accessories that were carefully coordinated by their moms. I see moms staying late to hand-make goodie bags and snacks for their kids' classes…when I see these things… I feel obligated to step up to the plate. They have set a social expectation that I could never meet, not without losing myself in the process. I sometimes wish I could be the everything mom, the super mom that cooks, cleans, works, sews, sings, plays sports, helps with homework, is fun to be around… Only cooks and eats organic, hand makes natural cleaning products, is earth and health-conscious. But oftentimes, when I try to

fulfill this unrealistic role, I end up falling into survival mode... I drive through McDonald's to get my son chicken McNuggets on the way home because let's face it... it's convenient, and it'll satisfy both needs... when I pick up a bulk box of goldfish crackers to give as classroom snacks on their birthdays because I'm just too wiped out to bake treats and wrap them up. When I allow them to watch Netflix on a Sunday afternoon so that I can roll over and get a 1-hour uninterrupted nap. Survival mode is basically lowering the standards I have for myself as a mom so that I can attain some sort of realistic balance."

I raise a toast to all those mums out there juggling your professional and domestic duties with tireless avidity. I'm awed by your strength and endurance.

Far too many women are relegated for not submitting to the maternity module foisted on them by others.

In her TED talk, Christen Righter said she chose to be sterile, but her doctors initially interdicted her choice: "*Having children was an extension of womanhood, not the definition... there are many paths to happiness and fulfillment. They all look very different, but I believe that everyone is paved with the right to self-determination... I want women to know... your choice to forego motherhood is not in any way your worthiness or identity as spouses, as adults, as women, and there's absolutely a choice behind maternity, and that choice is yours and yours alone.*"

Going childfree has gone global.

Bella DePaulo, Ph.D. wrote in *Psychology Today*. "*In the U.S. and other industrialized countries around the world, the number of women who postpone having kids, or who get to the end of their childbearing years without having any biological children, is on the rise."*

Are these childfree women selfish? Who's *"going to take care of them"* in old age? Don't they want to pass on their legacies? When I say, *"I want a child, somebody to take care of me, and carry on my name,"* what do you hear? I hear *"I—Me—My."* Now *that* sounds selfish.

Acclaimed author and parenting sage Dr. Shefali Tsabary, Ph.D. said parenting has *"elements of selflessness in it, but the driving force to have a child comes from your own desire to complete something within you."*

Having kids isn't *"foolproof insurance"* against growing old alone, per Dr. Shpancer. Some marsupial men still live and hide under their mamas' skirts! Expecting a child to take care of you later in life—is that love or enforced duty?

I was told a baby constitutes a complete human being, and without one, a marriage is a farce. I believed it. I went as far as thinking it'd be my bargaining chip for a boyfriend to stay. I thought if I raised some illustrious cherubs, they would obliterate my grisly childhood and have me outclass those women without little Joeys of their own—as if they were secondary to those with strollers. Then life threw me a curveball, and I looked at my impulses for shepherding a child. I realized I had no business to have one.

Kids are sentient beings, and Dr. Tsabary warns us about projecting our inner scarcity into them: *"Our children are not the jewels you get to adorn yourself with to mask your emptiness, and your children are not your puppets by which you get to fake an authentic life."* Dr. Tsabary advises against placing that burden on their shoulders.

I'm not making a case against parenting; I've just had a bellyful of being told I *"should"* have kids and being asked to work other people's holidays because I don't have any. I can defer being a parent, pave my own inimitable path, and still be a person of value in my own right. Having a child is an ability, not a responsibility. Creating life is a choice, not a purpose. Preschools and playdates aren't mandatory. Can you respect my individualism as you would your own?

Where is it written that women are supposed to *want* kids? Who drafted these outworn norms into dogmas anyway? To be childless by choice—*not* by dilation and evacuation or curettage—is to exercise autonomy, regardless of gender. It might be gutsy—hemming a conducive life exactly to your liking—but you're nobody's copycat. You're in control of your destiny more than you realize.

Please, sensibly propound the subject of motherhood.

Dígame, when you ask me and/or newlyweds, *"Don't you want a family?"* or *"When are you going to have kids?"* are you implying something's missing in my life or in their marriage? Or connoting a family only comes in one form?

Stop creating such urgency for others to reproduce because you're *"getting old"* and *"want grandkids."* Even when offered with the best intent, prodding a woman (*or man*) to pop babies because *we* want to be godparents, aunties, and uncles only serves our senescent agendas—not theirs.

If you tell me, *"Look at your cousins, sister, so and so— they have kids!"* know that I have my own life, and have no intent to mimic theirs. And of all the things I seek to find meaning in my life, your maternal suggestion or permission isn't one of them.

If it's ok to tell a woman who opted out of motherhood that she'd regret her decision, is it ok to tell a pregnant one that she, too, would regret hers?

Moral equivalence, anyone?

I've resurveyed my priorities and the rubbles I've survived, and in the present, I don't feel that same ebullience about parenthood as I once did. I'm past my reproductive prime, and there are warning of chromosomal abnormalities with advanced maternal age (*it's not a eugenic statement; it's a fact*), and my parental probability is now dim at best. In twelve years, I'll be a curmudgeon, asking for the senior discount. I'm content on my own and grateful for what I have and where I am. I don't have a *need* for a baby. I'm living my best life without one.

My phantom neonate shall remain unborn as a faraway follicle—a Zen-like zygote—who blesses me with freedom to sleep for twelve hours, nurture my career, marvel at new hobbies, and recreate myself when things get stale, without having to rearrange my life.

As my priorities change with time, I can (*and maybe I will*) reappraise having a child.

And in 2017, I did. There was someone. A man of God. Fantastically mannered. Successful in his chosen field. Our uncanny similarities were intoxicating. He was everything I'd never known and all I'd ever aspired to. He asked, *"If you find the right man, would you have children with him?"* With him, my answer was an open-hearted *"Yes."* But would life had been different had I not let the truth go by in silence? He could've been that one swell exception. Oh Laaaaawd, we could've made some beautiful babies.

My choice to not have children is neither peremptory nor permanent. If I change my mind (*I can do that, you know*), there are over 400,000 kids in foster care in America, and over 153,000,000 orphans worldwide.

A child isn't an item I can return to my uterus within thirty days with a birth certificate receipt if I were to realize *"I'm not cut out to be a mum!"* I'd rather change the course of my destiny with discretionary, non-biological avenues than be strong-armed into creating a life I didn't want or worse, terminate one.

We may not always agree on when life begins as we do when it ends, and I don't know why if I were to terminate my pregnancy, it'd be an abortion—but if my baby and I were shot on our way to the clinic, a double homicide. The shooter may go to prison—not knowing he/she didn't need to kill my baby—I wanted to do that myself. And strangers with stethoscopes in the E.R. would try to save a life—my baby's life—not knowing its own mother—me—just a few minutes before, tried to end it.

It is a life—otherwise, why try to save it? Or need to kill it?

With abortion, I believe there are very good people on both sides (*misconstrue that statement if you'd like*). Different choices and beliefs. Speaking *only* for myself, someone once photographed with an *"All about me"* shirt, if there's ever a time to think outside myself, it's pregnancy. It's not about aborting *my* body, it aborting who's *in* my body—I'm 100% sure it's of the human species, not of a jellyfish. In or out of my womb, I don't believe in dismembering any child: a six-week embryo; a sweet sixteen; a juvie eighteen. I don't believe in killing an invalid, braindead, bedridden geriatric (*a stage of life*) who's inconveniently dependent upon me or a helpless, innocent fetus (*also a stage of life*) who's dependent upon me—even inconveniently.

Rape? Incest? I know they happen 1% and less than 0.5%, respectively. I know the child has 0% chance to survive if aborted, but if given one, the child could have a meaningful life. I know of this one child—born of rape *and* incest—who wanted to be a writer—and she became one.

12. DINNER AND A MOVIE

"Life is either a daring adventure or nothing."
- Helen Keller

Nine-year-old smurfs shouldn't be watching PG-13 movies, but when *Dirty Dancing* debuted in 1987, my grown-up, voyeuristic cousins ogled at Patrick Swayze—and so did I. They swooned at his electrifying and hypnotic portrayal of the wayward dance instructor Johnny Castle. Starry-eyed, I had to sneak out of my room to gawk at the on-screen heartthrob—my jaw to the floor. My *"hungry eyes"* saw him, and my fixation with bad boys was born. One peep at Johnny and I knew I wanted to be with someone like him. Recalcitrant. Risqué. Mysterious. Outspoken, street savvy, charmingly uncouth. In and out of the dance floor, he's titillating and sensuous, but didn't take shit from anyone—not even his woman. Hold on to your knickers, *muchachas*! This troublemaker will ferry you to a cabin rendezvous, seduce you with carnal vulnerability and tenderness, then whisk you away and out of your element with eroticism and a musk of masculinity.

Give *me* the watermelon!

If he also smokes cigars and rides a motorcycle like the original bad boy James Dean, take me away! I'm gone!

As a true dork, my conceits of love are based on movies and music: *The Notebook* downpour kiss; *Cruel Intentions* elevator ride; *Notting Hill* press conference; *An Officer and A Gentleman* ending; Glenn Mederios' *"Nothing's Gonna Change My Love For You"*; Lionel Ritchie's *"Hello"*; and of course, Taylor Dayne's *"Love Will Lead You Back."*

For as long as I can remember, I've fantasized about being with a hardworking man who'd 1) know his purpose 2) live a life of honor, service, and integrity 3) take me out of my comfort zone 4) show me how intimacy feels (*think of Top Gun's pulsating love scene*) and 5) be my avenger when it matters most, when I need him most, and heroically tell the world how terrific I am, like in Johnny's immortal trope, *"Nobody puts Baby in the corner."*

After a few relationship tries at bat, I'm zero for five.

The starts of my relationships replicated the schmaltz of a Nicholas Sparks movie, and the ends, the combustion of a Quentin Tarantino's, with *The Bodyguard* soundtrack, and *"Just Once"* by James Ingram. By and many times before our sophomore year, I knew what we had had been all but possible. Like a loan interest, I've locked and lowered my standards in search of *"the one,"* but still missed the mark. I've forced intimacy to get a swash of love out of someone, made snapped judgment, repackaged patterns, and recycled excuses. Very green of me and very obtuse.

I did meet my Robert Kincaid (*The Bridges of Madison County*) and had *"The Time of My Life."* A carnivore, but a peregrine all the same. Just one touch, and I was *"anything but a simple woman"* losing my inhibitions. Today, I'd tell him, *"Wherever you're flying, come back. I'll be waiting for you,"* (*Aloha*), but we know how things panned out for Robert and Francesca.

In this post-game montage, I recapped my stories, not as a respected authority on love, as I've done everything wrong for most of the time, but as an ordinary woman who'd been plucked from the sludge and spoilage and found blessings among them. I scanned back these lessons and hope they'd instill hope in those battling in love and coping with losses, and help you recommit to what you stand for, who you are, and what you want.

Help yourself.

♡ Top 7 things I learned from dating ♡

1. *"Love when you're ready, not when you're lonely."*
- Former monk Jay Shetty

After divorce, coupling seemed to be the currency and holy grail of happiness on social media, and anniversary dates evoked an assortment of dreary feelings that made me even more painfully aware of my singleness, so anyone with an Adam's apple was attractive—and I wanted to boff them. I was a basket case. I wasn't in the right headspace to think above my loins or outside my trousers—or beyond the next hour. At the alp of loneliness, a male companion would've been revitalizing, but me in a hookup—or a relationship—would be like trapping an asthmatic kid in a carpeted room, teeming with cats. No thanks, hard pass.

With the help of Doritos and tubs and tubs of Rocky Road ice-cream, I learned how to choose patience over instant gratification. Use another human as a means to an end? To scratch an unfulfilled itch? It'd be devious to make a petri dish out of someone, hoping love would sprout out of it, or a guinea pig cowboy to test if you're ready to giddy up again. It would not be my first rodeo (*I'm grimacing as I say this*), but I couldn't do it again, not in good conscience.

2. *"Don't make long term decisions based on temporary emotions."* - J. Shetty

In *The Breakup*, there was an invisible scoreboard on who could move on faster post-split. Want to meet your next *"Forever best friend "*? Like, now? Go on Hinge! Tinder! Happn! Then Voilà! Rebound nirvana! Rapid recuperation! Must be kismet! You're walking on sunshine! A quick fix, a quick relief, a quick seat filler turns into a twelve-month lease because slow and insipid pace won't create airbrushed Facebook images, but a scurry to the altar will inarguably outdraw and garner congratulatory points. It may allude to moving forward, but the jaunty image is one-dimensional. When the frolicking fizzles out, you're flummoxed why they don't look so foxy over morning cappuccino.

Alacrity and ardent love mark the advent of a relationship, but long term decisions are for the long haul. The thrill of a nascent relationship can desensitize just about anything, but do you want transitory, band-aid fixes or a commitment for eternity? A take-out soulmate doesn't exist—fast and fresh flavors delivered to our door within minutes. Chemistry is good; compatibility is best. The innumerable permutations of compatibility go beyond *"How do you like your eggs?"* Pull the brakes, Derby. Better to lag in the right direction than to sprint in the wrong one. The right person may be en route, if unhurried.

I've long preferred a long-lasting connection over a second hand, short-term substitution, so my pathos-filled, asexual interim was about healing—not rebounding. I've never had much game anyway.

3. *"You can't heal until you feel."* - J. Shetty

If thoughts or talks about your ex still kindle lovey-dovey feelings or are rankled with microscopic traces of anger or smidgens of other distasteful emotions, like irritable bowel syndrome or heartburn, there's still healing to do.

> *"If you don't heal from your past, you'll bleed all over your future."* - J. Shetty

Buddhism welcomes suffering as ingredients of life. I liken them to an unbidden visitor, a superbug with no accelerated *"medical miracle"* vaccine. In my eagerness to preclude pain, I missed opportunities to learn what I needed to learn.

Where I left off with a previous relationship was precisely where I picked up with the next—in pain.

With every guy, I told myself, *"If he really loved me, he'd stay."* Then there I was, splayed on a clump of debility and tears. If a man would've wanted me then, I'd tell him, *"If you really loved yourself, you'd leave."*

I've pushed the pain aside, but it kept revisiting me until I heeded its lessons. I had to make friends with my demons. Heck, I had sleepovers with them and singly learned their names: fear; grief; anger; shame and its second cousin guilt. Like out-of-town guests, they needed space and time—lots of time—to unpack. My demons and I had peace talks, and we didn't fill in any silence. Through emotional awareness, there was a rollout of who and what instigated my pain. When we integrated—not with fright or judgment, but with compassion and understanding—they left and excavated the emotions that'd been smothering me.

As the Persian proverb said, *"This, too, shall pass."*

There's no right way to hurt, but you need to live it out. If you give yourself a romance moratorium, take time to not be fine, sit in that discomfort, weep, and be inundated with tears, you'll see there's meaning in suffering. You can look for a sorcery, but unless you delve into your problems, they won't fix themselves. Start with bitesize doses and bitesize revamping. Just start! It's a scrappy middle, a tempestuous interlude, but keep going. Ascertain if there's air in the tire and if you have the bandwidth for a fledgling relationship. Work from the ground up; from the inside out. Once you metabolize pain's purpose, you can ultimately discharge it to where it belongs—the past.

4. *Rinse and repeat.*

Do you feel drawn towards the same kind of person over and over again? I did.

Douglas LaBier, Ph.D. of *Psychology Today,* wrote, *"We see both men and women repeat old patterns because, for example, their own unresolved conflicts and dysfunction remain unconscious and therefore re-enacted in one failed relationship after another."*

Why do men act like they could walk on water? I don't know. I just had a habit of dating those who did.

Why did I put myself at the mercy of these noncommittal, overgrown babies? Why did I give more than I could and more than I should to these romantic cul-de-sacs? Why did I create problems when there weren't any? Conclusively, guess what I didn't have?

A study by the University of Toronto showed a strong tendency to be drawn to parallel *"types"* of personality. Dr. Douglas LaBier suggested, *"The key to liberation from this pattern is growing sufficient self-awareness about it."*

Ding, ding, ding! Self-awareness—the cognitive espresso.

5. *Do NOT settle*

How I wish I could coax everyone to stave off this mistake at all costs. I get it—I would've settled for a low-budget remake of *Dirty Dancing* to find my Johnny Castle. Or make a Faustian pact to find someone close.

I know settling like a bishop knows the Bible. I know how to set the bar and stoop to a new low. I know what it's like to sacrifice truth, fervor, and vehemence for a safe second best. I swung for the bleachers, but struck out. Couldn't get a homerun? Bunt and settle for a steal. Flabbergasted with deflated desirability, I felt I couldn't find anything better, and the ones out there are way worse. *"Better to be with the wrong one than no one,"* I thought. Anyone, please, *"Love me, love me, love me"* (*Bruce Almighty*). In loneliness, I ached for human touch, and the 14,000,000 photoshopped, glossy pictures, *#relationshipgoals,* pestered me to settle for whatever Gremlin I could get, believing it was the best I could do.

But in knowing your worth, you realize *"for now"* is an ill-fated substitute for forever. Settling for anyone to have someone is beneath your dignity and below your potential. *"There are plenty of fish in the sea"* holds a nugget of truth. You do have bigger fish to fry. You just got to stop fishing in infested water, and cast a wider net. Refuse to settle. It's an act of self-love and self-respect.

6. *Step away from the Keyboard*

Your ex has someone new, and you're now in a snare of nebulous thoughts: How'd they meet? Is she a skinny slut? A fat floozie? A boob-shaking bimbo? A high-maintenance hussy? Did she go to college? What kind of job she has?

So, you think you're a *Peeping Tom* for spying on the new girl's profile?

Hold my beer.

Like Gigi in *"He's Just Not That Into You,"* I've been *"on the precipice of staging a casual run-in"* and *"drive-by."* How else could you know if your ex moved to Amman, Jordan and taught math? Or became a patent examiner, ran for his town's City County, and lost? Or married an older woman with almost the same last name as you and moved into a three bedroom, two bathroom house in Santa Clara, California? Just me? Fine.

What's good in stooging around the Dupont Circle metro in Christian Louboutin five-inch stilettos, a tacky keyhole top, and a tawdry leopard miniskirt, during inclement weather at 23:30 (*when the ex and his new girl leave work*)? Or by the Franconia-Springfield metro at around 08:00 (*when they leave home*)? *Nada*! Yet, I've cyber stalked my exes, their new girlfriends, fiancés, wives, their parents, siblings, in-laws, and Jiminy Cricket.

Other stuff I did were—uh—marginally litigious.

In relationships, I was vaguely aware of who I was, but preoccupied with knowing who my partners were. After a breakup, it was all about knowing—more like encroaching on—the next girl. Like Gigi, I fanatically checked social media *"at fifteen-minute intervals,"* encased in a cobweb of comparisons: her locks vs. my pompadour; her cheekbones vs. mine. Is he treating her better? Is he happier?

They can see you snooping on their *"stories,"* you know?

Yeah, I didn't get that memo!

"Hi, I'm JG, and I'm an Instagram stalker."

Like a cheetah to a gazelle, I was irredeemably inattentive to everything else, much so that my friends said I needed an *"Insta-vention."* My bestie Clay exorcised that demon when he said, *"You're my best friend and I love you… just walk far away from this situation as fast as you can."*

> *"In three words I can sum up everything I've learned about life: It goes on."* - Robert Frost

They were right—the obsession occluded me from moving on, and I couldn't be unclogged until it's nipped in the bud. If I was going to be obstinate over a reconnaissance, let it be about me and my unexamined life, my unchecked ego, and my unsolved inquests. Every click, every comparison, every rewind stagnated and plundered my joy and my chance to reset. The focal question was not *"Did they find someone better than me?"* That's external, and it can be amplified with liquid searching. To quote the movie, *"It's amazing what ten shots of Patrón will get you."* The question is have I become better without them?

It's explicable; we've all done it. According to a Norton LifeLock poll, 46% of Americans have stalked their current partner or exes online, and 9% had created phony profiles to check their social media. Phony profiles? Gross! I didn't do that! That'd make me a creep, which I'm not—really.

7. Sweet-Talking Romeo

"I will never hurt you." "How did I get so lucky?" "You're the one." "You can trust me." And the mantra of younger men, *"Age is nothing but a number."* Heard them before?

And the whopper, my favorite: *"You're my priority."*

If you hear any of these, be an audio engineer, and do a sound check with facial recognition software. Strap them to a polygraph, bolus them with sodium pentothal, get a urine sample, and interrogate them. I emphatically endorse that.

These suave big-talkers and their bewitching presence and beguiling personalities could (*almost*) woo everybody, and sell a dildo to a nun.

My emotional intelligence meter was always stuck at room temperature, so I fell for whatever they said—not what they did. These men seemed inerrant, and I would've traded my life for theirs. I heard violins! The birds were chirping! Lay me down on a bed of roses! Eureka! Euphoria!

First, promises—it's like being with Casanova. Then alibis, lies, whereabouts, and confessions—like being with Nixon.

But like Anna Scott, "*I'm just a girl, standing in front of a boy, asking him to love her.*" I'm a stickler for pillow talk, so I heard what I wanted to hear. Had they told me they could turn water into wine, I would've said, "*Oh wow! Red or white?*" Albeit there was a cornucopia of clues, I was too enamored, too gullible, too transfixed with their garbled apologies and excuses to see the sinister signs blinking like neon lights and conduct any detective work. Whatever line they fed me, I gobbled up. It was symbiotic degradation.

Here's your cinematic checkpoint.

Does Romeo suit your specifications? Is he a man who wants to build a future or just a boy who loves to talk?

My message: be prudently optimistic *and* be assiduous in sweet nothings. I'm a downer, but a discussion without demonstration makes any man like all other men. If they show you they're dubious, believe them! If they show their impure interiors, don't repaint them!

And those statements of real significance: "*You complete me,*" (*Jerry McGuire*); "*You make me want to be a better man,*" (*As Good As It Gets;*) "*My heart is, and always will be yours,*" (*Sense & Sensibility*); "*I'll be your husband,*" (*The Great Gatsby*). Believe them?

To my visual learners, anybody can promise you the world, but pardon my incredulity—until they deliver, it senseless.

Let that sink in.

In the spring of 2006, I was buttoning up my contract at Stanford hospital. I couldn't wait to return to the East Coast to start my next travel assignment—Manhattan. I asked my friend Joe for a recommendation letter.

Flashbulbs on Joe for a second. What makes him an *akamai* (*smart*) and substantive pro, far from other flaccid leaders? At bedside, if a patient's in V-tach, dyspneic, hypoxic, or hyperglycemic, all I care about is if Joe knows whether to grab a nasal cannula or a non-rebreather, the Amiodarone, Insulin, or Narcan, and can he draw up the correct amount with either a 3cc or 1cc syringe without a calculator before the patient turns cyanotic—then return to managing a 912 bed, level one trauma hospital. He can—and he did. I don't give a bleep (*and it's none of my damn business*) if he's a Caucasian male who identifies as a mango, diversifying the nursing quota, raised by a pangender mother, a pansexual father, or an albino dolphin. *¿Entiendes?*

Back to the recommendation letter; I told Joe it could wait.

I'd stay in Palo Alto, then I was off to Portland, Oregon.

I told him something like, *"I'm loving California, but Portland's enchanting! Friendly people, fresh air, no taxes, and subways! Weather's unpredictable, but I love vagaries! I love rain! And oh, mother nature! There's Multnomah Falls, Astoria, and lots of rose gard-"*

"What's his name?" Joe couldn't listen to my nonsense much longer.

I placed my heart squarely on my sleeve, and my friends (*not only Joe*) took notice from 6,000 miles away. I thought an upright man was in short supply—a commodity—like a VCR, Betamax, an objective journalist—so every manhunt for Mr. Right had been a hurtled misadventure. I was either infatuated with a guy or trying to get over one. I navigated around the same pitfalls, hounding for the next corporeal antidote for loneliness.

It was the dude I met on the Hoover Dam. He lived in the beaver state. Much like the storyline in *"Fools Rush In,"* I *"can't help falling in love with [him]."* We even listened to that song while on the dam and ate at Gray's Papaya. Our epoch was a race to romance. It must be a Vegas voodoo. He said I was his muse, and in less than two months of fervid dating, I reorganized my timetable, my career, and my life for this guy. His name was Mr. Wrong.

There were all named Mr. Wrong.

13. NOW AND MAYBE FOREVER

"He's more myself than I am. Whatever our souls are made of, his and mine are the same."
- Emily Brontë

Engagements last between twelve to eighteen months on average in the U.S., and destination wedding is a burgeoning market (*Hawaii is second to Vegas*), with each costing around $28,000. Around 2,000,000 wed every year, budgeting a bit over $35,000 each. Only 3% of brides are agreeable to get a prenup, and 80% change their names after marriage.

Nurses have a 28.9% divorce rate.

I'm another statistic. If there were a category for myopia over men, I'd be up for an award. My relationships would be laughable if they weren't tragic. Dating. Engagements. A called-off engagement. Marriage. Divorce. Been there, done that, got the T-shirt. I'm a cautionary tale, so if doling out this list could reroute you from such fate, let's have it.

Take it under advisement or not.

♡ **Top 10 things I learned about marriage** ♡

1. *Don't ever—EVER—buy your own engagement ring.*

That is all I'm going to say about that.

2. *Marriage isn't a coronation.*

Married. What does that adjective tell you about me? Or other ones we now seem obsessed to use to catalog people: bisexual; lesbian; trans; binary; single; divorced; black; white; green; purple; blue? Is any or all of these an **earmark** for a devout or unholy person? If you file your taxes? If you wash your hands after #2? If you stop for pedestrians?

Being a "*Mrs.*" didn't make me a prig or put me above the food chain's single coterie or make me more of a woman than the rest. I went to work, paid the bills, took out the garbage, wolfed down an Ambien, a Benadryl, or both, and slept my dilemmas away, like everyone else.

I didn't access into a jewel-encrusted throne as Queen Bee who sauntered past the single paupers once I said, *"I do."*

I was JG—married, not coronated.

Why do we put the wedded on such a pedestal?

If you feel subaltern for being single or think marriage is an indispensable pointer of adulthood or the culmination of life, I implore you to broaden your consciousness, and rejig your tunnel vision.

3. *Marriage a commitment – no shit.*

This I thought I didn't need reminding, but often forgetting.

When things go sour, lovebirds don't post their decrepit marriage on their profiles or park them in their garage. Do you believe their lives are as astonishing and adventurous as the intricately styled anniversary reels they post?

I wish I'd reoriented my lofty expectations of marriage.

In my estimation—for all its legal weight, sizzle, warmth, and comfort—marriage isn't as glamorous as the single enclave thinks it is. As it turned out, marriage is neither an assurance of happiness nor a testament of worth.

When the honeymoon reached its acme, when playtime is over, and oxytocin levels waned off, the real work began.

4. When choosing your partner, think bottled water.

In 1995, this gigolo picked me up in a Corvette for a date. We strutted down D.C.'s opulent Georgetown area, feeling demure and spiffy. He ordered seafood, steak, and scotch. The check came; Liberace *"forgot"* his wallet (*what is it with me and men with amnesia?*) He asked, *"You want that last shrimp?"* As I was paying, this bootleg baller asked if I wanted a nightcap. He didn't know his homeboy Raj was my coworker whom I debriefed beforehand. I knew his job and income bracket. I knew he borrowed that Corvette from a friend. I knew he lived with his mama. I wanted a free meal, but there was no way in hell I'd go home with him.

Thank God for Raj's free background check!

Aside from his work (*hey, a job is a job*), my date was a hop, skip, and a jump away from a *"scrub."* Do we need a TLC refresher course? Well-funded is not the same as well-sourced. I see the fascination with a bad boy—a wild card. But a joker? Check, please.

Lesson of the story: like bottled water, when it comes to your *cariño's* finances, lifestyle, temporal treasures, and swagger, know its source. Comb out the real story like a *CSI: Miami* Investigation. You'll spend the rest of your life with this person, so do your homework. No Mata Hari. No Trojan horse. What are you (*not*) willing to live with?

Want to have a family with someone who still depends on his/her parents, the ex-spouse, the baby mama? That house, that car, that bling bling—what (*or who*) is its provenance? Know if it's responsibly sourced before flaunting it to folks and on the internet. My forwardness may offend you, but I know of *no* self-respecting woman who would if it wasn't.

Exhibit A:

5. *Mine is mine; yours is mine.*

A prenup won't taper your bra size by a cup or emasculate his manhood by an inch, but it will protect your chattels. It's a controversial and unsexy topic, but mooting over the niceties of *"who pays for whom"* is far less bellicose before you have your first dance.

If neither of you will treat the marriage license as a lottery ticket for one and a debt certificate for the other, why not have jointly beneficial protection of each other's respective funds and properties? Why not put it in writing?

There's a prenuptial agreement and a post one. If properly executed, both are legally binding.

Relationship expert April Masini said, *"You'd have to be crazy not to have a prenup before marriage… you insure your car, your home, your health—you should ensure your insurable assets against divorce."*

Christopher Elliot wrote in *Forbes*, *"A prenup clarifies your financial rights and obligations, offers protection from debts and settles property rights before you get married."*

If divorce happens in light of yesterday's recession-reeling, pandemic smitten economy and today's inflation, without any legal ban, your ex can monetize the marriage. Your ex can bankroll you to pay for his next.

Do you want to learn from my mistake or yours?

6. *Don't expect the grass to be greener on the other side.*

I got married hoping to find happiness and completion; I got divorced not finding neither (*I'm a killjoy, I know*). My message's somber, but to expect happiness from a partner is a grandiose quest. It's an unfeasible venture for anyone. It's no one job to make you (*or me*) happy or alleviate your insecurities. It's setting them up for failure.

Jay Shetty wrote to his wife, *"You are not here to make me happy; that's my responsibility to make me happy. You're here to support, enhance and add to anything I do, and I'm here for the same."*

I was married for six and a half years, and in that short time, I learned that had I worked on myself first—my own internal freak show—I could've intrinsically experienced happiness and radiated it from within. Our dalliances can't create it for us. Our lovers could crank up the volume, but we need some starting materials for them to work with. They can't start at zero. As self-aware, self-respecting, self-loving, self-caring, (*notice how they all begin with "self"*) individuals, we wouldn't be a burden—we'd be a bonus.

Everybody wins!

Until you're clearheaded about what you can bring to the table, you might want to hold off on the date and the venue.

7. *Slackers and Six-Figure.*

Attention: six-figure, two-comma paychecks *Reinas*, if you have disposable incomes *and* your men want to step up, let them! I'll have what you're having!

Your love might not cost a thing, but medical, visual, and dental coverages do.

In his *New York Times* bestseller *"Act Like a Lady, Think Like a Man,"* Steve Harvey wrote what I've seen firsthand. He said, *"Tell him straight up: 'I need you here to protect and provide for us, give us security in our lives, to help raise these children."* Profess, protect, provide, and *"If they're doing anything less than that, they're not men."*

And my personal favorite: *"Boys shack. Men build homes."*

Patience, love, nurturing, loyalty—all the gifts that only a woman in love could give. I know you got this, but who got you? Don't let a brother grow complacent! Make room for him to court, impress, and provide for you.

Your lucrative career isn't his hall pass to be a sloth. It's a partnership, not a payoff. A good man of whatever income or age will not loll around because of those extra zeros. Lay down the ground rules, and say them out of the gate.

If chivalry is dead, resuscitate that motha!

8. *Take your blinders off.*

I don't normally do feelings, but for a shoddy shot in love, I've let it hover over logic. Presentiments were there, but I rhapsodized the pluses, shriveled the minuses, and skulked around the sketchiness, so every guy looked like the alpha and the omega—a knighted second coming of Christ. When I was no longer inebriated from the keg of romance, I took the red pill, and it was clear as day—I was catfished. Why is reality such be a buzzkill?

Lesson: we all have our own peccadilloes, and they don't stop to exist just because we refuse to acknowledge them—married or not. Why constrain them? Like a lotus blooming from muddy waters, partake in each other's unfurling.

9. *If it doesn't work out, get a divorce!*

> *"I've been afraid of changin' 'cause*
> *I've built my life around you."*
> *- "Landslide"* by Stevie Nicks

With the divorce, I didn't just let go of a lie—I let go of a life. My husband *was* my life.

I was aghast when asked why I thought divorce was so dreadful. *"She's the one who wanted it!"* they said. And that makes it painless? Divorce is anything but! It's soul-crushing, and so is its indignity.

Would you ask a widow who hoped against hope and took her comatose husband off the ventilator, *"Why are you mourning? You're the one who did it!"*

If you think marriage is just parchment, *"just a piece of paper,"* try uncuffing yourself from it lawfully through a text or email.

10. *It's better to be single—wishing to be married—than to be married—wishing to be single.*

Read that again.

VI – TRUE BLUE

"You have enemies? Good. That means you've stood up for something in your life."
- Winston Churchill

14. TWO + TWO

"No one is more hated than he who speaks the truth."
- Plato

January of 2018 was a dour month. My Hawaii friends roster whittled down to two when my ride-or-die chick Regina moved to Japan. Reg was my work buddy; my Pollyanna. This hottie is fashionably late to everything, she waits two weeks to return a call, and can turn a monotonous conversation into hours-long cacophonies. Don't be within an earshot of us when we're bumbling follies and guffaws, and simultaneously, we shouldn't be on speaker-phone.

A year before that, in November, I had a karaoke jamboree with Regina and the gals for my thirty-ninth birthday. With December forthcoming, Reg asked if loneliness had crept up on me. I said it did—and it also had taken up residence in my bed. What transpired next changed the tenor of our talks for years to come.

Whenever this diva begins her sentence with my name, she ain't flippant.

"JG, you blindsided Carlos with a divorce in September. October, you didn't party with anyone. This month, it's your birthday, and you're alone. Next month is Christmas. Who's going to kiss you on New Year's Eve? Then February, you'll be alone again on Valentine's. Seriously! Who wants to be alone on their birthday? Divorce during the holidays? You couldn't wait until March, Boo Boo? I don't know what happened 'coz you still won't tell me, you bitch. Things must've been so shitty that you felt the need to get out the way you did."

You *"follow the science"*? Can you follow the math?

Regina has two Master's—neither in math—but in favor of logic, this sexy siren collated information with her heart *and* her head. With common sense, she deduced that when her best working theory was added to the joyous cloak of marriage I've paraded in public, things just didn't compute. She'd seen the divorce settlement (*it should've had a gag order*), the emails, etc. Reg knew the chronology of events belied the barrage of untruths that circulated in Kaneohe, Waikiki, and Waipahu, and these gibberish bred suspicions when taken in their full, expansive context—they were as legitimate as a Louis Vuitton purse on Canal Street.

Reg knew the numbers were in dispute, the disparities were irrefutable, and the veracity of the story ran much deeper.

How was the truth subtracted from the equation?

"It's incredible the way you start the story in the middle."
- The one and only Dr. Thomas Sowell

When the optics are odious and a man's back is against the wall, peer perception axes personal integrity, he forgets his honor and tenets, and the periphery between the two gets hazy. He palliates his guilt by corroborating his innocence and modify his stories to make him a saint, others, sinners.

We are more of what we hide than what we show.

When only prejudicial evidence have probative value, when opinions and lived experiences are told as *"my truth,"* and plurality of opinion as *"their truth,"* when dipsticks believe they'd been told to drink bleach, and gunshot victims aren't prioritized in Oklahoma hospitals due to *"horse dewormer"* Ivermectin overdose *(Nobel Prize, "essential" human med per CDC, NIH, WebMD, and FDA)*, we've lost the art of truth-telling—and people will believe just about *anything*.

I've heard, *"The Devil has many tools, and a lie handles them all."* Some people wear it like a second skin. Honesty is also a tool, but one very few can handle.

There are impostors and masters of manipulation—the first could improve their truth-telling skills, given all the hoaxes they propagate, and the second can depict their enemies in a diabolical light. Both dissemble as much as they disclose. These Pericles of perfidious babbles will stab you, stitch you, then tell the world they saved you—while pinpointing to themselves as victims of circumstances. They'll crochet the textiles of their stories to make themselves look like scarecrows turned heroes. So crafty at winning acceptance. So carny with powers of persuasion. So guileful at gaining public sympathy.

Those pricks with figurative reflex hammers will poke and prob you, ram your patellar tendon to send a signals to your quadriceps' stretch receptors, to your spinal cord, and back to the alpha motor neurons of your femoris muscle, thus innervating an impulse, causing an excitatory contraction. *They* perturbed you to kick, but chumps will believe—social media will believe it was *you* who kicked them!

Get it? Congenital liars!

When I called the police on one such prick who defended my ex during the divorce by hunting and harassing me—twice—saying, *"to[o] bad you did [Carlos] like that,"* and I should *"leave the island,"* among other repellent remarks, his mom said she didn't understand *"how this is escalating into a bigger issue. In our lives this has been resolved."*

So, all was good in *their* life, and it was I—*minding my own damn business*—was the one making things worse.

> *"Recognize the game before it's being played."*
> - Political commentator and lawyer Ben Shapiro

When blemished characters are at risk for exposure, forget the unvarnished truth. People will lie to you and about you, smear and vilify you, launder facts, besmirch your name, feed you to the hyenas, rip your heart out, then stomp on it.

And then there's us—mortals innately inclined to agree and protect our own by reflexively mediating to their defense.

Psychologists call it *"observer justice sensitivity."* We get worked up by the callous treatment of others without (*any*) direct involvement or observation of the events. We throw accusations in punitive haste, misapprehend what we hear, opine impolitic and nonobjective judgment, side against the supposed rival without empirical attestation, and soothe and commiserate the ostensibly guiltless, injured party—even validate their victimhood with a microphone for the whole world to hear. Tell me *"your truth,"* lovebug!

> *"The redefinition of truth to mean anything I like, and the redefinition of falsehood to mean anything I disagree with is a dangerous thing."* - B. Shapiro

Sometimes, the problem is neither the muted nemeses nor the crisis. It's tech interferences, misperception, misprint, the misconstruction of facts and opinions, and the airheads renaming these terms. When the facts don't fit the feelings, the truth becomes a narrative violation—a credibility crisis.

Of the many things we tell ourselves and others, it's the truth we don't always accept or entirely deliver.

> *"A lie can travel halfway around the world while the truth is putting on its shoes."* - Mark Twain

For example: Did you hear I disallowed my ex from going to his bachelor party? Or I *"behaved"* to win him back and *"bugged"* him at work that he *"had to get away"* from me? FACT CHECKERS! PAGING THE FACT CHECKERS! How about I got a nurse fired? Or I was so belligerent to the personnel of a local establishment that they installed an *outside* camera, should I return and accost them. No *inside* camera to invalidate my infamy? They said because of my *"mental illness,"* I couldn't understand *"[their]side,"* and I didn't go by the book. Bitch, I *am* the book! Want to see (*their*) redaction at its finest? Go on Yelp, read all about it!

Rumor mills run on steroids with juicy, lachrymose stories. Loose lips are at large; listeners beware. Open mouths and close minds are guzzled by gossips' gravitational pull. I've learned that nitwits who know least say the most, and those with the most to hide whale others for the very things they do. These douches should be reincarnated as suppositories.

People don't hang their dirty laundry on Twitter when their egos are sundered, but their sore and temperamental hearts will get a bullhorn, huddle up their delegation, and spew an earful of tirades about their foes. If they do unclothe the unjust, it is to enumerate the indelicate acts done to them, (*not what they did to others*), posture themselves, and slant their stories towards sunlit angles for condolences.

Cry me a river.

It's all part of their modus operandi: thoroughly omitted sections; beefed-up discrepancies; cunningly falsified add-ons; dialed down delinquencies; positive spins on scruples.

> *"We accept a story uncritically if it confirms what we'd like to be true." - "What to Trust in a Post-Truth"*
> by Dr. Alex Edmans

Stories aren't objective; our cognitive colanders sieve them to duplicate our beliefs and theories. Hearing them is only getting a spoonful of someone's selected story bites—not a full meal. We could be misfed by a half-baked lie, so don't preordain it as gospel truth. No matter how resounding the oration, how vociferous the speech, it's still one-sided.

But we've all been there—one version, one perspective—and we fall prey to the perils of partial presentation.

During the divorce, I wanted to divulge my story, but too enmeshed in pain, I'd be doing it out of pique. Ever met a fair-minded, disgruntled ex? Better to hush while you heal. I lamented privately and offloaded to a few I thought were discreet—regrettably, it ricocheted. It was futile—staying below the radar. Illusive remarks got transmitted from the grapevine, through coconut wireless—some misinterpreted, some expurgated, some invented, and *all* unconfirmed.

> *"When you don't know the facts, you resort to lies."*
> - Judge Jeanine Pirro

Flagrant lies—and *chismosas* did just that—and then some. Circus of obnoxious allegations and hearsays. Inflamed by spurious and unilateral stories, social media became fertile ground for opposition firing squads. Incited by conjectures, cretins meddled in my business, embellished, and injected themselves as relevant in my story, in service of their own. My ex told his friend he couldn't *"handle [my] shit,"* any longer that he's *"getting a restraining order against [me]."* The most farfetched was this nutjob who had the audacity to call his apartment my *"sanctuary"* during the divorce and threatened to file lawsuits against me for *"trespassing," "homophobic slur," "defamation of character,"* and causing him and his partner *"sleep deprivation"* and *"emotional distress."* All talk; no action.

My individual misconducts were derived into a sweeping generalization of *all* Filipino women. They were murmurs that it wasn't the boys—the women were the lunatics.

It was amateur night, and ties with these meathead severed and bifurcated. Oh, the credulity of idiots. None informed, but all opinionated.

Any Beavis and Butt-Head could make allegations in the kangaroo court of public opinion. Evidence be damned! In the case of the people of paradise vs. JG, dum-dums played judge, juror, and executor in unanimously incriminating and convicting me for these charges: one count of spousal abandonment, one count of Facebook infidelity (*check out my Halloween "hunk" of 2017);* one count of homophobic slur; two counts of vandalism; and three counts of being a psycho—unmedicated and disfavored. Penalties: intrusions and harassment that took two restraining orders to quash.

I've binged on *Law & Order: SVU* enough to know that even the most heinous criminals have the right to face their accusers (*the last scene of "The Undiscovered Country" is worth a watch*). These ignoramuses acted as if they had ringside seats to The JG show. I was pissed, but why take my rightful turn to confute the marital mischief drivel—and be acquitted—when the whole island already bought the lies of its ringleader?

Playing victim? It's so unflattering. And it's getting old.

> *"Some things are believed because they are demonstrably true, but many other things are believed simply because they have been asserted repeatedly, and repetition has been accepted as a substitute for evidence."*
> - Dr. T. Sowell

Don't believe him?

Turn on the tv, pick a few consonants, maybe a vowel, and see why less than 30% of Americans find credence in the media, and of the forty-six countries surveyed in worldwide news trust, the U.S. came last per a Reuters Institute study. Remember Lafayette Square, June 2020?

> *"Facts do not cease to exist because they are ignored."*
> - Aldous Huxley

If you don't like your landlord, but he calls, saying smoke's coming out of your window, would you ignore it because of how you *feel* about him? You deride that loony geezer! Cookie conspiracy! I bet if you'd wish you'd found out the truth if you found your home incinerated.

> *"Facts don't care about your feelings."*
> - B. Shapiro

Stick to the facts. Always.

When we stack the deck against someone, predicated on a canard or a crass opinion of another, our attitude towards that person is swayed—tampered even. Without awareness of our own bias, even a preponderance of evidence will be erred as misinformation or disinformation (*whichever shite fact-checkers call stories they don't like to defend the ones they do*). Without panoramic, areal knowledge of the facts, casualties get caught in the crossfire when we shoot in open range. In a nutshell, if it's not your story, you only have snippets—save collateral damage.

A tip: not knowing the truth is not analogous to not wanting to know it.

Of all the simpletons who made a spectacle out of me, *none* had the decency to confront the alleged enemy whose name they've tarnished through back-channel chatters. I thought at least one was going to ask for *my* side of the story.

> *"I wish a motherfucker would!"*
> - Cedric the Entertainer

I would've summoned them to the kitchen table, and my menu—peppered with proofs—would've sliced and diced the cooked-up revisions they've heard and disproved all the filleted fabrication they've been previously fed. Entrées: a luscious logbook garnished with digital trails; fruity drinks with footages; and deglazed dossiers (*if only bodycam and wiretapping were permissible*). Desserts: salacious secrets frothed with delectable surprises. Oh, their whetted taste buds would've drooled for more...

What to do if a discussion is too menacing?

> *"Surround yourself with people who challenge you, and create a culture that actively encourages dissent... appoint someone to be devil's advocate."*
> - Dr. A. Edmans

Find someone fearless, maybe apolitical, to challenge your supposition or—I'm saying this with aloha—you can also just butt out. If you're teetering between a tug of war of facts and fiction, it may be sensible to stay on the sideline. Picking sides and switching sides are irresistible methods of allegiance, but they can exacerbate the feuding. If you can't be Switzerland, don't chime in your speculating voice to an already existing truth-deaf choir.

If the altercation involves mutual friends, back down. It's about them—not you—no need for a liaison or an emissary. I know, *"Bro's before ho's,"* but whatever you heard could be a ploy to poach you, poison your view, and/or cut you off from the other person. Jesus had apostles, but liars have accomplices—and believing a lie can be as harmful as the lie itself. It's one thing to listen—another to agree. Friends offer consolation to both and cast contempt on neither; they don't ascribe blame or tear one down to build up another. If you value both friendships, opt for impartiality.

> *"What we share is potentially contagious,*
> *so be very careful about what we spread."*
> *- Dr. A. Edmans*

Don't mire someone's prestige with a flurry of discourteous keystrokes just to be virally *en vogue*. If you only know half of the story, don't put it on full display.

I'm not anti-story; I'm pro-truth. I'm an exponent of it. Through the pain of exclusion, I've learned the truth is typically shrouded from the headlines and/or obscured by omissions. I've learned the pernicious effects of one-sided stories—they're alienating and infused with venom. They egg people on to autopsy someone alive, and dissect where things went wrong, and who did what. I've only known them to disband peace and never to institute it. If we grant them primacy, we perpetuate their predatory ripple effects.

The infectious power of communication is best used when creating connections—not trampling the truth.

Storytelling, if done by a schmuck, is an instrument—don't let it play you. Any disconnect in its dynamics is worth calling bullshit on.

While everybody has the right to his/her own rendition of events, nobody's ever squeaky clean or wholly culpable. Every story has three sides: his, hers, and screenshots. The truth is somewhere in between.

If you think finding the truth is gripping—and it is—and it matters more than any narrative, go Columbo. If you want to throw the first stone—don't—but if you must, take your surmise, rummage through the intel, and siphon first-hand knowledge from second-hand information and actions from reactions for a 360-degree diagram of the truth. Before you believe the buzz, pop the hood. Plausible deniability? Any manufactured data?

You might dig up some dirt, lapses in integrity, crinkles in the story—even the clincher.

And if you still believe 2+2 = 5, bless your heart, Sherlock.

If you've been the butt of the joke of inequitable stories or you've lost support because of them, no worries.

> *"Three things cannot be hidden for long:*
> *the moon, the sun, and the truth."*
> \- Gautama Buddha

If you want to sue someone, or you think they're trying to murder or defraud you, don't start an online contagion of accusations. Put proof where your allegation is! Go to the cops; file a report. No anonymous sources, no anecdotal affidavit, no emotional suggestion. See if the evidence can sustain your charges.

> *"When you make a statement, you got to back it up."*
> - James O'Keefe of *Project Veritas*

When my ex-husband got engaged (*legal term: "change in circumstances"*), it was chronicled on Facebook (*God bless the evidential use of social media*). I stopped sending him support (*$1,000/month*), but he said he still *"need[ed]"* the money—shocker.

As cited in *A Few Good Men*: "It doesn't matter what I believe; it only matters what I can prove." I invited him to prove to the judge—not to me—why I should *not* donate the remaining tranche (*the remaining thousands of dollars*) to animal rescues and shelters because he—who just bought a swanky, 1.03 carat, D, oval and marquise diamond—needed it more. Unless he had *"reasons other than to take further advantage of me & have me pay for both [his] wedding,"* per my email. Bank statements, receipts—I'd show mine if he showed his. I *never* heard back.

> *"Until the lion learns how to write,*
> *every story will glorify the hunter."*
> - An African adage

On that note, should you want to vitiate my stories—any or all—or have me undergird them, my contact is in the back. I'll do *"Yes," "No,"* who, what, where, when. I have dates, places, times. No preselected or softball questions; no non sequitur or ellipsis; no binders or notecards. No cackling or unnamed sources. Grill me or quiz me—hell, bring in Peter Doocy—you chose, pumpkin. I won't circle back.

15. THANK YOU, DON'T COME AGAIN

"A true friend stabs you in the front."
- Oscar Wilde

Untrained employees are unusable during a medical emergency called *"Code Blue."* It's set off through an intercom—a rapid response to a critical case. Respiratory and cardiac arrest would urge the use of this panic button. The hospital's All-Star team—the heroes of the clinical world—blitzes into the room and thwarts the patient from atrophying—stat! It's graveyard precarious, so bring in the big guns and a crash cart containing practically all life-saving apparatus, drugs, and handbook—whatever they can dispense from their arsenal. Those in the hallway lengthening their necks like giraffes just *"to see what's going on"* have no vital function. Their superficial support serves no therapeutic value. A hardline is drawn between who needs to stay and who needs to go.

Only a few are helpful. Only a few are essential.

I looked like a zombie and stunk like one in the throes of divorce—drenched in teardrops and upchucks. I flatlined, and my friends—my defibrillators—brought me back to life. The tourniquets who averted my hemorrhaging. Like a public health disaster, I needed urgent, around-the-clock care, and someone was on standby at all times. Some per diem, some overtime. At my lowest ebb, only a few proved to be helpful. Only a few proved to be essential.

When the dominoes fall, and you're off the grid, swirling into Armageddon with an avalanche of agony, you'll know who won't give up on you. When you're overwrought with your sanity lurching away, they'll buoy you into salvation. When you're at the gallows, looking like a sobbing gook, they'll be your guiding light, walking alongside you. When you're not who you are or where you need to be, their arms will keep you steady until you're no longer beyond pathetic recognition—these compadres are champs of dependability.

When you coil down a cyclone, they'll jump in, no matter the depth, cauterize the bleeding, stay until you're out of the woods and have the faintest signal of a pulse.

"Not on my watch," they'll say.

Hurricane JG arrived on the wings of my divorce.

I was so wracked with grief, it was visceral, and to say every second was excruciating would be an understatement. Cloistered and waxen, I erected a jailhouse, bolstered the locks, closed the shutters, welded new windows and bars, and kept the world out and myself in.

It took an intersession from Jesus, Mary, and Joseph to begin the most elemental tasks of self-care. I vegetated for hours, slept for days—nutrition negated. Heavenly laden, I dragged myself out of bed to swab the crusted, tear-stained snots off my face—and that was me in good shape. When washing's exulted as a small win, you're pretty far gone—gone off the rails. I couldn't live through another gruesome minute, much less another day. I had nothing left; no place to turn. My reserves were slashed. I needed a kickstart.

Like Steve Jobs outlined in his email to reconstruct Apple, I needed *"all hands on deck"* to move me out of a monsoon and keep me afloat until God quit picking on me.

"Lord, if You can't salvage me, send someone who could!"

As the tide turned, God did dispatch a battalion of angels with unparalleled loyalty and solicitude. In them, I saw the hand of God and felt His mercy. They kept me from going under and out of the crosshairs. Compelled by compassion, they didn't split at the first sign of trouble and offered hope with unflagging empathy. When I ran away, they followed. When I swam upstream, they were a thunderbolt of succor. When I needed silence, they gave me space. When I didn't know which way was up or how to find the middle, they met me at the bottom. Every step of the way, there was a surplus of solace, ready to bring me home.

Their deeds—not words—tilled me out of the ditch.

My friends didn't know each other well, some not at all. Most had never met and didn't live in the same time zone, but their loyalty to me was what they had in common. Their presence, virtual, across state lines, or in the flesh, was their gift. They called and asked if I was ok, and in characteristic propensity, I said my catchphrase, *"I'm fine."* I was lying, and they knew it, so there was no beeline to my Broadway show. Like pulleys, they lifted me back on my feet and to the dog park, Sunday mass, and island hopping. We did movie marathons, miso, cupcakes—even quietude.

No impersonating Freud or claiming to have superpowers to expedite my healing. I did the legwork for that.

Most of it was hand-holding and showing up to say, *"I'm here, and I won't forsake you."* I didn't need them to solve my quandaries; I needed them to show me I wouldn't face them alone. Nearness to someone's crisis can be daunting, but at my very worst, they gave me their very best.

Case in point: a month after my divorce, my Manhattan pal

Virgil visited, and while we were ambling around Waikiki, an acquaintance asked him if he was vacationing. Virgil said, *"I'm here to jump-start this one."* Virgil was also my jumper cables who quarterbacked my search and rescue in 2007, 2008, 2009—you get the picture.

The unerring test of friendship is uncovering who'll stick around when life and all its beauteous and blackened layers go south on you. You can call yourself a *"friend"* and pass that off as a baseline standard for loyalty, but when I need you, and I get crickets, what good is your absence? If I must look under every nook and cranny, beyond brambles, and under rocks to find you during my time of need, you're not a friend—you're a letdown.

And what a crappy way to show you care.

Friends are like undergarments—they provide support by staying put. You can't embolden a fragile friend when you look for the nearest exit when they bowled over the zero to shit scale. It discredits the very foundation of friendship. With today's technology, how could anyone go radio dark? A terse text can go a long way. A hug is affirmative action. It's better to have a starter boost than none at all.

Disclaiming a friend when life capsizes is like telling your houseguest there's no room in the guestroom. It's a one-two gut punch. To not respond to a friend's outcry or not help extenuate their predicaments is to extinguish the light at the end of their tunnel.

When friends are in their most harrowing hour, it's really not the time for verbal palsy. *"I don't know what to say."* But if you *did* know, what would it sound like? Don't plead ignorance with "*I don't know what's going on."* No need for 411. Your knowledge isn't needed, your presence is. *"I don't want to take sides."* Bravo! Don't take sides! Take actions—blatant actions! Don't just go rogue—not with these cop-outs! They're nothing but elaborate escapes and handy excuses at their best. They're as credible as the twinkie defense.

If I were to list all the excuses I've heard, it'd take me all day: *"I meant to call you, but…";* *"I wanted to take you out to coffee, but…";* *"I've just been so busy."*

Yadda yadda—say no more.

Nice touches, but they all rang hollow. Demonstration and intent, don't confuse them—the first *says* something good about you; the second *does* something good to others. Leave your flaky, unconvincing excuses and one-liner, feel-good platitudes at home.

I've said it before, and I'll say it again: intentions without actions is lip-service loyalty—and I make no distinction between enemies who shoot men in the back and troops who leave their own men behind.

What to do with these no-calls, no-shows? I'd tell them to go sit on a cactus. You pull an exodus on me today, you're obsolete tomorrow. Not catty like me? You can take their silence and nonappearance as the rowdiest and clearest message to release those relationships. They've run their course. They've served their purpose. They're complete. They were there when times were good and *only* when times were good. If their idea of friendship is tagging you on their barhopping pictures during your most disquieting hours, *Sayōnara!* You don't need them—their falsehood is certified. Unsubscribe and release. Unfollow and release.

Unfriend and release. File them under *"Missing Persons,"* and close the case. No love lost, only lessons learned.

What if they block you, and you become a social pariah?

I cleaned house when my divorce took a turn for the worse. *Arrivederci* fugacious friends and backstabbing fruitcakes. The move was summarized as *"You guys have been there for her, and this is how she treats you… it's her loss."*

My loss? Let me explicate this concept to those hooligans with an I.Q. of a hotdog: just because you were always there *with* me didn't mean you were there *for* me. Getting rid of imbeciles who couldn't catch this contrast wasn't a loss. I'm infinitely better without them—and with greater peace. That's a gain.

Block away, bitches! Your digital barricades don't halt my blessings. Palling in comparison to the short-term loss in popularity was a long-term gain in self-respect. The lesson I've learned the hard way: when a bullet narrowly missed your heart, you don't give someone a new cartridge to get the job done right the next time.

When someone pays plaudit to *"I'll be there for you,"* (*Jon Bon Jovi*) but pulls a Houdini when shit hits the fan, that's friendship fraud—counterfeiting to do A when in truth, you're doing B. Frankly, I'm done with this. Faux friends are as dud as a three-legged stool.

If you or a loved one have been a victim of friendship fraud, call 1-800-GET-LOST.

When you bounce back (*and you will*), and Johnny-come-lately reappears from the woodwork, tell him/her, *"Thank you. Don't Come Again."* What was fuzzy is now in the foreground. Thank you for the widescreen enlightenments: faithful friends find ways to stay; fickle ones have a garden variety of excuses to leave; enemies don't betray you, loved ones do; truehearted friends don't dispose of their loved ones, disloyal ones do when they could no longer use them; friends can have their personal objections over your choices and still support you if they bite you in the ass; friends give and friends receive.

And those who have your back are best situated to stab it.

Most of all, those who don't know the cost of betrayal will *never* know the value of loyalty.

And today, loyalty seems to have a devalued currency—like love, reliability, impeachment.

A whack from an enemy is much less malevolent than a kiss from Judas.

The *Harvard Study of Adult Development* is the longest longitudinal research to date, and according to its fourth director Dr. Robert Waldinger, M.D. *"Those who kept warm relationships got to live longer."*

Colby Itkowitz from *The Washington Post* wrote, *"Casual relationships, like the ones forged on social media won't do; neither will contentious ones like an abusive marriage or an unreliable friend."* Itkowitz reported Dr. Waldinger *"consciously reach out more to friends who are sick or struggling, even if it feels uncomfortable, because he knows how much that connection will mean to them."*

There's no worth to equate or price tag to put on having people you can count on when you're down and out. Get on board with this and appraise how satisfied or dissatisfied you are with your relationships. Your sphere of influence is sacrosanct, so upgrade them (*if needed*) as regularly as you do your phone, and watch your life optimize.

I scaled down my public life and zoomed back the lens of my connections; I was fastidious in reshaping, triaging, and paring down these domains and whose privy to them. My trusted circle is small, but sturdy—password: loyalty. Its boundaries are airtight, its proponents, handpicked. Quality over quantity. From time to time, we have diametrically oppugnant views, but they stood by me when I felt like a human piñata and proved themselves worthy of inclusion. These united few have been vetted. The disingenuous, fair-weather loons who served no legit purpose were ousted. They're parachutes that malfunctioned during my airdrop.

> *"My friends are my estate."*
> \- Emily Dickenson

Mine are my soul guardians, my lifeboats, my solid rocks. They carried me past the debris with love and conviviality, one tornado after another. This army of angels didn't make the turbulence go away or less spooky, but they buckled me during the ruckuses and cushioned my fall. It's an honor to find these increasingly rare and invaluable friendships that have become my assimilated families. I know where their loyalty lies and how far it goes. They have mine as I *never* had any misgiving about theirs.

If it's my loyalty you want, you better goddamn earn it.

As social creatures with inbuilt dependence on each other, be watchful of your own turf, flush out the decoys, traitors, and moles, and be scrupulous in choosing who watches your six, and who gets the boxed seats and the bleachers.

Impose a stipulation against treachery—an entrance fee in the form of fidelity. Friendships are volitional, and if they can't get behind your pal screening program, find someone else who can.

Personal evolution behooves us to rename the roles of those in our lives and to recast our social order, appropriate to our standards. Different acts call for different roles. We arrive at each novel scene, armed with new knowledge and new priorities, and when you've outgrown your shell, each stage needs new faces.

Be intentional with bridges you cross and those you burn. You're a glorious fusion of Care Bears and cacodemons, brutes and butterflies, sheen and squall, rainbows and drab. A true friend wouldn't cherry-pick which parts of you to nourish and which to neglect.

I pray that when life takes you for a downward spiral—as it does to all—even through no fault of your own, you'll have a crew for collision control.

I got mine. You better get yours.

VII – PURPLE HEARTS

"I am only one, but I am one. I cannot do everything, but I can do something. And I will not let what I cannot do interfere with what I can do."
- Edward Hale

16. LAVENDER

"Spread love everywhere you go. Let no one ever come to you without leaving happier."
- Mother Teresa

Nanay Belen's *champorado (Filipino chocolate rice porridge)*—nobody could ever hold a candle to it. My grandmother was colloquially referred to as *"Nanay Belen"* by those who knew her *(Nā-nāy is Mother)*, but she was *"Mamang"* to me—a moniker I made up as a kid (*I made up all sorts of weird shit when I was a kid*). I remember leaving dirty bowls in the sink—her pet peeve—her ravishing tribute to Queen Helena of Constantinople as Queen Mora during our town's *Santacruzan*, how she loved Air Supply, and how she kept our home spotlessly neat. She lathered and folded our clothes so immaculately, they looked like pressed sheets, embalmed with a quaint scent.

Lavender—her favorite fragrance.

Standing at only 4'10, she was dainty and diminutive, but profusely mobile and spry. She'd raised two children, five grandkids, and more than thirty nieces and nephews. She did as much, if not more than our own parents. No adult was too slovenly or Flintstone too petulant for her angelic patience, not even the naughty duckling whose many antics included shoving a peanut up her nostril (*guess who?*). She didn't have favorites, but if she did, it was I—duh (*I got her heirlooms*). She was most elated when surrounded by her *"magagandang apo"* (*beautiful grandkids*).

Mamang was by our side when we took our first breath, up to when she exhaled her last.

But with our great grandparents—our potentates—not so much warmth.

The Garcias were Victorian in their treatment of others and the adulation of their own brood. It had nothing to do with blood and everything to do with money—their golden calf. Prominent, profane, morally dilapidated. Almost t loveless. Depending on where they placed you on their totem pole of preeminence, you were either family or footman.

Mamang was a scion of this family, but she didn't have an avaricious bone in her body. She married a provincial man with a menial job and little education—like herself. Such being the case, Mamang was expendable—the least favored among the children. She was sent to be the caretaker of her younger siblings and nieces—like their indentured servant. Though treated as an underling, Mamang labored hard with an amenable heart that was never defiant.

Mamang was also a single mother who toiled away at every imaginable job to put food on the table. She knew thirst; she knew hunger; she knew hard work.

I remember the smell of ginger permeating her *tindahan* (*store*), where she sold *lugaw, arroz caldo, pansit palabok*, and *dinuguan* for ₱50 a plate. Her dishes were so delish, they sold out in a jiffy! Pennies after pennies, she saved, bought, and helped build the 7,600 square-foot, orchard-filled Garcia compound. Our family had partitioned it for themselves into adjoining abodes—*walang pagod, walang hirap* (*without tiring, without difficulty*). This is how one person—Mamang—had changed the lives of many.

Can't say they'd taken prudential care of what was handed down to them.

Neither her face nor name is plastered on postages or on seminary pews, but Mamang was a pylon of compassion—it was her abiding trademark. Servile, unassuming, ascetic. Even without much, it was she who gave more than most. With repleted stomachs and spirits, families and neighbors scarfed down her food, sought her *na'auao (wisdom)*, and felt better than themselves in her presence. Growing up, this was a workday sight at home. Mamang looked into people—not at them. She was our miniature Dali Lama.

When hearts were indurated, Mamang did what medical interventions couldn't do: she softened them.

This was her gift: a lifelong practice of altruism.

When it comes to espousing the holy scripture, Mamang was twice the person I'll ever be. Her piety to Christ was the bedrock of her beliefs. She relinquished her life to His will with her dedication to relieve the burdens of others. She felt called to connect with the poor and had an affinity with the ill and the suffering. Mamang had a fondness for all animals and valued every form of life with tantamount passion. She fed, bathed, clothed, and housed people from all walks of life. The most humanitarian person I had ever known—with no close second. Six years after her passing, we still reminisce and revere Mamang as an epitome of compassion—someone close to a living saint.

Governed by God, she could do no other.

> *"Every man is guilty of all the good he did not do."*
>   - Voltaire

Here in America:

- over 158,000,000 men live in poverty

- There are about 15,000 homeless people in Hawaii.
- In 2019, there were 37,085 homelessness veterans.
- 1 in 7 children live with hunger.
- More than 40% of us can't pay a $400 medical bill.
- In 2019, there were 47,511 suicide cases.
- 9.7% of youth has severe major depression.
- According to the World Health Organization, stress is *"the health epidemic"* of the 21st century.

I know the predominance of stress. I've moved in and out of depression, monetary strain, and physical instability (*the list goes on*), not knowing how to find my way home.

There are over seven billion people on earth—why is there an outbreak of loneliness? Could it be because the rich and famous are deified as celebrities, and those with substance abuse and mental illness are classified as wackos?

But simple acts of kindness can make human predation feel defanged. And to me, compassion did more.

How about spending $86 million of taxpayers money on homeless vets, living in squalor, put them in hotels with free meals and on buses to see their families or on those injured while enforcing the law by those who break them? The bereaving families of American heroes who'd fallen at military posts and the laid-off Keystone pipeline workers—they could use some of that money.

Give alms, patronize charities, assuage the disenfranchised with art, campaign for the cessation of human trafficking and animal violations that reek of perversion, help dispel myths about addiction, or just be nice to others, irrespective of spiritual preference or sexual orientation. The more you reach out, the greater the value of your philanthropy.

Mamang sang "The Star-Spangled Banner" flawlessly in spite of her choppy English. I was awestruck! That's when I learned her story... Born in 1928, she lived through the aftereffects of Spain ceding the Philippines to the U.S. and that of the Filipino-American War. When Philippines was an American protectorate, she had to hymn both the U.S.

and Tagalog anthem in school. She called foreigners who came to the island in 1937, "Mga galing sa ibang bansa." They were Jews fleeing from the pogrom of the tyrannical scourge that was Hitler. Philippines had a president then, Manuel Quezon, who had the moral courage to make his country's message clear: Philippines stands with Israel. Together with transcontinental efforts from American cigar tycoons, the Frieder brothers, U.S. envoy Paul McNutt, and Colonel Dwight Eisenhower, Quezon helped 1,300 Jews escape the Holocaust and find refuge and housing in the Philippines. He wanted to protect more, but on 12/8/1941, Philippines was bombed by Japan. Mamang was 13 then, and she remembered life besieged by Japanese hegemony. Beheadings, lynching, beatings, starvation, enslavement, Babies bayoneted, families lived in bunkers, men riveted to bamboos, forced to glug gallons of water until they ralph, then disemboweled upside down, carnage, girls and ladies kidnapped to be "comfort women"; sexual slaves, routinely raped in front of their husbands and/or in a hostel called "The Red House." After the U.S. attenuation and conquest of the Japanese regime, after the Bataan Death March, and after the Manila massacre, Philippines was liberated, and its sovereignty was recognized by the U.S. on July 4, 1946. After German Nazism and Japanese fascism, Filipinos and Jews were free. Mamang spoke of these persecutions and invasions with misty eyes and never a dollop of hate. She didn't get to see the Open Door monument in Tel-Aviv—a symbol of gratitude, compassion, and brotherhood between Israel and Philippines—but she made it to Lady Liberty.

Got a van? Shuttle our *kūpuna* (*elders*) to their pharmacies or to their appointments. Got money? Buy them groceries or their prescriptions. Got time? Babysit for free.

In a country of proliferating chaos and rampant insurgence, where cities look like bonfires, racial tolerance and equality are smokescreens for riots and ructions, revolts are chalked up as a political end, eunuchs abdicate their civic devoirs in subverting their clout to cronyism and corruption, dystopia and divisiveness, and vandals menace communities and get commendation, so long as raids and anarchy are perpetrated as allyship, I see compassion cascading into extinction.

Must I not believe my lying eyes?

When a body is in the morgue—someone's husband, wife, son, daughter—is it compassionate to say, *"Rest in power"* to those you like and *"Rest in piss"* to those you don't? Is it compassionate to tell God He should've taken somebody else? To think this is the ripe time to have disquisitions on collegiate women sports or election reform or crack down on gun confiscation? Is that compassion?

Or is it decaling their names on jerseys and lionizing them as martyrs when—and only when—they look like you?

When Angelo Quinto, a Filipino Navy vet, was cuffed into submission and died three days after a cop knelt on his neck for nigh five minutes in December 2020 (*mainstream media?*), should I visit his family, crump on others to say his name under compulsion, remonstrate, rappel effigies, anoint him with murals as the next San Lorenzo Ruiz, seize on his death as an omen for brown people to *"live in fear"* for it *must* be Asian hate, plan the most resplendent funeral cortège, and thank him for *"sacrificing his life"* under the canopy of compassion because—and only because—he looked like me? And the cop who asphyxiated him doesn't?

Would there be compassionate and unending airplay to demand justice for a white man from Rochester, NY who died after being deliberately engulfed with ignitable fluid by two black teens, or a twelve-year-old white boy from Pittsburgh, stabbed inside a McDonald's by a black man, or a Pakistani Uber driver who was tasered, carjacked, and killed by two black girls, and two white ASU students who were told to leave by two black students *"because this is [their] space... and [their] white!"* if—and only if—the races were reversed?

Compassionate feminist? Got a -D after your name? Ok! #metoo #imwithher #believewomen

Got covid from a *"sophisticated"* party in the Hamptons? Monoclonal antibodies for you! Got it from an event with American flags? Die, grandma killer! It's how we ration compassionate treatment now, right? Unvaccinated—die, should've gotten your shot. Pneumothorax—die, should've worn a seatbelt. Esophageal cancer—die, human chimney.

I recall a Senator's compassionate declamation: *"When we have children crying for their mothers and fathers, don't you dare call that 'border security.' That is a human right abuse,"* and *"When elected, the first things I'm going to do... is shut those private detention facilities."*

Kids who'd been kidnapped, smuggled, raped, and flung by cayotes over a fourteen feet fence are now sardined in those squalid, overcrowded *"migrant facilities"* that are 1,700% overfull—where two Yemenis terrorists tried to cross—where 18% of families who did cross have covid—where over 7,000 positive cases were released at the border with 30% vaccine refusal—and where 14,000 Haitians are under a seedy, ramshackle overpass in 100° C weather—unvetted, dehydrated, and unvaccinated. And that Senator is now the second highest-ranking, female official in America.

I've seen the operatic compassion shown to *"kids in cages"* who were *"ripped from their parents' arms."* Where's that hammily compassion now? For both sides of the border?

Where were the presidential tweets, the flotilla of activists, the crocodile tears, and the kabuki theater of compassion for Natalia Wallace, Daniel Shaver, Tony Timpa, Jeremy Mardis, Linden Cameron, the 264 police officers killed in 2020, and the 13 dead soldiers from Afghanistan? A life lost is one too many, but I guess who took it matters more.

Rob a Macy's? Sure, these people *"have insurance."* Burn a police station, acid on police, *"they probably deserved it."* Unruliness in Kenosha, Atlanta, Chicago, Portland, Dallas, Minneapolis—it's social justice. A cop killed one unarmed woman, and Congress reconvened hours later on 1/6/2021, insurrection! Insurrection! Insurrection! *"The worst attack on democracy."* January 6 criminals belong in jail for their wanton acts—so were those on 7/24/1998, 11/7/1983, 3/1/54, 9/11 (*2,996 deaths*), and 12/7/1941 (*started WWII*).

My lying eyes tell me a virus isn't the only pestilence in this country: there's caucus based compassion and ideology based indifference.

When sociopathic hoodlums don't get the verdict and/or vote they want, they tread over the safety and civil liberties of law-abiding citizens, spit and thwack men and women in uniform, ransack mom and pop shops, and graffiti homes.

Nothing shows you're conduit of love like looting a Fendi or Gucci or you're an ambassador of peace like $2 billion of *"mostly peaceful"* pillaging. Nothing says life matters like an average spike in homicide by 37% in thirty-four major U.S. jurisdictions—including de-facto warzones. And it's underhanded to bail out bandits with fundraisers.

Coddling criminals is not compassion; it's a propaganda push.

This entropy bisects the third world country where I was born from the perilous one I live in, but hardly recognize.

There's never a greater need for kindness in human history than now. Dispiriting matters of preponderant magnitude loom over the welfare of this country and yonder, yet had we gotten so political that we are prudish?

If compassion is meted or withheld contingent on who's in—or out—of the White House, which narrative is trendy, or which rebellion is rife, we're neither compassionate nor nonpartisan—and it's ineffectual to avouch to be both.

Someone in your life could use a helping hand—high or low. But before you stir up nationwide goodwill, mobilize change for the less fortunate, or decide to be a courier of compassion by preserving peace, or purveyor of incivility, ask thyself if your amity awareness has an asterisk.

> *"You can't legislate love."*
> - Denzel Washington
> (*My second favorite actor*)

Because we're people first, politicians, etcetera, second. Because compassion doesn't have to come with a caveat. Because love is compassion by another name.

> *"The opposite of love is not hate; it's indifference."*
> - Nobel Laureate and holocaust survivor Elie Wiesel

> *"Indifference elicits no response. Indifference is not a response. Indifference is not a beginning; it is an end. And, therefore, indifference is always the friend of the enemy, for it benefits the aggressor—never his victim, whose pain is magnified when he or she feels forgotten... Indifference, then, is not only a sin; it is a punishment."*
> *"The Perils of Indifference"* - E. Wiesel

I've heard if you're having trouble making yourself happy, make someone else happy. I tried it—it's a win-win.

And with all the soporific reclamation of healing and unity, what are we to do with the rest of our mortal days? Convert oxygen to carbon dioxide, peacock every mundane moment with a grandiloquent selfie, and take up petty space because theoretically, it's inimical to no one? Like a narcissist?

> *"Under the sky, under the heavens, there is but one family."* - Bruce Lee
> (*My birthday twin*)

One family under God—not one bureaucracy under two polities.

When was the last time you gifted someone without return or did something humane and sought no reward? Instead of being rude to everyone you don't like or squawking racial hang-ups to those you don't agree with, why don't you rise above the politics, leverage your gifts by being a beacon of light to someone suffering in the shadows, and extend a hand of friendship to someone down in the rut.

Do something heartfelt that actually advances civilization.

If you're going to invoke the powers of innovation—the intersection between technology and humanity—do it for widespread harmony—not ego enlargement. Match your electronic popularity with a purpose, and draw traffic on humanizing situations that make us vulnerable. Leave the fact-checking to the tech overlords—as they always do. If you're going to make history—miniscule or otherwise—make it a good one.

Compassion is a deep well that must be full before it can overflow to others.

Usher in self-compassion.

> *"If your compassion doesn't include yourself, it's incomplete."*
> - Psychologist Jack Kornfield, Ph.D.

It's unheralded to some, so think *"copy and paste."* We say tenderhearted things to those feeling unworthy of love and lenity. When they wallop themselves, we remind them of their wellbeing. This is the compassion template we are to apply to ourselves. Tune out the self-bashing; recognize you're human—you fail, and you fall. Go easy on yourself.

Too many feelings, not enough facts?

Here you go: Serena Chen of *Harvard Business Review* said, *"In recent research spearheaded by Jia Wei Zhang, we discovered that self-compassion cultivates authenticity by minimizing negative thoughts and self-doubts."*

Marie Warrell of *Forbes* said, *"One study of students found that those with higher levels of self-compassion were able to handle disappointment more positively and stay more motivated to keep trying after their failures."*

My grandma used to say, *"Maligaya ako pag nakakatulong ako,"* meaning *"I'm happy when I'm helping."* And she did with such gladness. Mamang was an earth angel—if ever there was one. I'd clone and canonize her if I could.

She taught me service seeks not to be recompensed, love is a loan without a payback, and compassion is a selfless act without an agenda. It's what you contribute—not consume. It's giving without banking any favor or presuming extra points, because when you take someone into your heart and a part of theirs heals, the joy of giving is its own reward.

For me, the reward is a whiff of lavender whenever I make someone smile.

The phenomenal work of the Potter's hand, our Nanay Belen.

17. MAN UP

"Never trouble another for what you can do yourself."
- Thomas Jefferson

Grocery stores in the Philippines sell bulk *Tsinelas (flip-flops)*. We're so accustomed to these rubbery polymers that they're the homespun footwear back home. Flimsy ones are about $2, foamy ones, $3. In 1996, it was much less. I was in Noveleta that year visiting my uncle, Mum's brother, my Tatay Mario *(Tāh-tie is Father)*. One day, his slippers ripped, but he didn't want a new pair.

He sat on a stool, pulled the pliers out of his toolkit, held the torn soles by his belly, and twisted the coppers wires around the splintered Y-shaped straps. It was like watching a luthier master his craft.

Within seconds, he's wearing his clamped, worn-out pair.

I had $2 to spare. Had he asked, I could've replaced them.

Tatay replied, *"Anak, bakit pa ako hihingi sayo? Tingnan mo, kaya ko naming yariin to."* In English, *"My child, why would I ask that of you? Look, I can fix it myself!"*

That's my Tatay—a man of unmatched stubbornness and integrity, who pulled his own weight, and rowed his own oar. His life wasn't one of ease, but of self-sufficiency and independence. He came from wealth, but was given a bad hand in life. He was loved less and chastised more. Due to his grandparents' nepotism, his relatives had milked every penny of their prodigal pedigree, but he got sloppy seconds.

Only in my worst nightmare could I had imagined when I would him see Tatay next.

Knowing this unfair world wouldn't hand him anything on a silver platter, he was utilitarian—solution-oriented.

Tatay never loafed around, waiting for someone to level the playing field or make things easy. He wasn't a freeloader. He didn't believe in free rides. No one was his backup plan or financial plan: no benefactor; no stipend; no surety—no monthly checks in the mail. He didn't blame his father for leaving them for his mistress or hate anyone who was better off than he—he didn't demand their transfer of wealth. He didn't depend on the Philippine government giveaways (*it's an oxymoron*). No Medicaid, free tuition, or EBT there. A self-feeder, who lived on what he made, and didn't tap out of his responsibilities. What he wanted and had in life, he got on his own. What we remitted to him, we offered.

He *never* asked; he *never* begged.

Nobody made a project out of him. Tatay was a machinist, an electrician, and a carpenter. He was truant, but keen and streetwise, with eclectic talents and experiences under his belt. If something's broken, he'd MacGyver it. He raised roosters and sold pigs. He also worked in construction in Saudi Arabia, and with his first paycheck, he bought me a dual cassette boombox. He looked for a J-O-B spanning across all disciplines. Some, no ample traction—not from lack of browsing—but lack of luck. For every uptick in the level of hopelessness, he doubled down on the upswing of self-reliance. Tatay was a titan with a spine of a ramrod.

When his chickens clucked and the coffee's percolating at 4 a.m., we knew all was set. He'd boiled enough water in his thermos to warm up five to six pails of cold water for us to use to bathe. He'd cooked breakfast for everyone using a single propane burner. Once we left for school, he hustled from sunup to sundown, driving his rusty tricycle to make ends meet—or cover enough radius to pick up passengers to make at least ₱200 to buy dinner—that's $4.

We had bunch of books, but not toys, so Tatay got creative. I was jealous of a cousin who had teacup-sized, motorized trucks—I remember feeling poor. Tatay gave me centavos, (*coins*) and I felt rich! (*I didn't know their nominal worth*). My *"cozins"* and I divvied them up, stuffed them in plastic bottles, and shook them like maracas!

With Tatay, music was our form of entertainment. He was an autodidact artist, he harmonized, and played the guitar and harmonica—but couldn't read an arpeggio.

I miss his baritone voice…

My favorite memories are of him strumming the chords of Eric Clapton, Sinatra, Elvis, and The Beatles.

This grade school dropout homeschooled us on individual responsibility, right and wrong, and hard work. He didn't speak like a politician, but he was truthful. He didn't hold one standard for us and another for himself. He didn't care if he was liked, but by God, Tatay was respected. He was an upstanding man of simple taste—an alphabet soup of credentials never won his good graces. Colonial mentality is still prevalent among Filipinos (*porcelain skin in, mocha out*), but even then, Tatay believed he was the equal of everyone he faced. Those who called him a recluse didn't know they've paid him a compliment. Because he ate from hand to mouth and drank from the industrious chalice, he knew the value of every drop. Tatay was muscularity and momentum, discipline and dignity, anchored in willingness to show up, and do the work. Even with abject privation, his strength remained in his ability to look after himself and his family.

What an honor to bear witness to such self-reliance.

Tatay and I on my first birthday. Mum said I was grouchy that day (and every day), and only Tatay could pacify me. This was the only picture of him holding a baby—he had four of his own.

I don't have the language to fully extol his true north, only that Tatay's probity was unimpeachable, and his principles, unrivaled. If gauged alone by his planetary belongings and stature, the math wouldn't be in his favor. His yardstick for the true goodness of a man was his inborn character—not where he stood on the rungs of power.

"Palabra de honor" (*word of honor*) was his bushido—one he ingrained in me.

As adults, taking care of our own needs is the touchstone of self-reliance. Only a leech would live off the marrow and fat of another, and vacuum all he can from anyone who can give. Nothing is sexy about taking more than you need. To rely peripherally for survival, instead of earning your own livelihood, is not only contemptible, it's self-smiting.

I'm well aware of my own restrictions. There were days I feared where my next dollar would come, and I borrowed more times than I should. These lessons Tatay ensconced in my psyche: don't bypass my own gumption; don't take advantage of others; and don't be dependent on sources outside myself. I'm alright with falling short when I don't have the means to do—not because I'm too feckless to try.

We all need *kōkua* (*help*) at some point.

What have *you* done that failed that you're now down to your last recourse? What was so far beyond *your* capacity that you must pass the buck onto another? What have *you* tried to fill your wallet before probing others'? Are people recycling the responsibility of taking care of your marsupial ass? Is your wifey infantilizing you into indolence? Need mummy to get you a Hot Pockets? A tampon?

Maybe between Nickelodeon, fingerpainting, and parmesan cheese, you could pull yourself up by the bootstraps, and make something of yourself.

An object at rest will stay at rest—that's physics. Once in a while, life barges in, change your velocity, and it'll feel like none of your efforts are landing.

No one knew this better than Tatay.

My biological father had gone rogue long before my birth, but his family thought he'd bequeathed his all to me as his only heir, so when they renounced me and my mother—in envy—we had no support.

Tatay Mario manned up, took us in, and raised me. Given his shortage in space and money, he could've shirked that *kuleana* (*responsibility*) and saved the measly supplies for his own family, but he never grumbled. He was the man of the house, and he did what he had to do to provide. Tatay made pallets out of plywood for the kids to slept on, and the adults were on the linoleum floor, with *Banigs* made out of handwoven palm leaves.

Making matters worse on the moorland, tensions between the Lintons and the Earnshaws (*Garcias vs. Delos Reyes*) bubbled over, my father continued whoring around, and his clan grew more rapacious. They did some unspeakable and hateful things to me and Mum—and by osmosis—Tatay's family was adversely affected. They cut off our electricity and banished us from our home. Destitute, we had nothing but the clothes on our back and some balled-up bedsheets. His mother-in-law had a farm—it was our refuge—where I learned to walk.

Picture the labor of transporting a family of eight—with a tricycle. No U-Haul back then. Just a sidecar and Tatay's elbow grease and feet pedaling us to safety—with just enough light from the moon.

He rolled up his sleeves and drove his tricycle around the slums and squalid corners of Cavite, under the scorching sun, for our daily bread. Tatay was tenacious and intolerant of excuses. *"Weapons of the weak,"* as he called them. Like uncle, like niece—he despised grown-ass men acting like impaired birds.

One night during a blizzard, I was out of milk. With low visibility, Tatay drove his tricycle (*his only run that night*) and came back with a lacerated instep arch. He stomped on the slippery footpeg to get the engine running, and the metal blades punctured his tissues.

I would *not* be here now had this man not broken his back that day—and every day—to keep me alive.

> *"It's better to die on your feet than live on your knees."*
> \- Emiliano Zapata
> Mexican agrarian rights revolutionary

Lowlifes auction their allegiance to the highest bidder when responsibilities stagger and provisions dwindle. At the feet of deep pockets—at the altar of conformity—varlets bow. Payouts and payrolls; profit over principles. These cowards and would rather bootlick for a drop in the bucket than get calluses in their hands—takers doing what's easy, ignoble, and undemanding. Don't throw them into a lair; they won't survive. Don't throw them into the lions' den; they cannot lead. Not every boy can be a man—this sets wolves apart from sheep. These takers and sycophants grow good-for-nothing instead of growing a pair.

Tatay told us, *"Magingat sa mga abusado. Bigyan mo ng kamay, kukuhanin pati braso."* He meant, *"Be vigilant of bums. Give them a hand, they'll take your arm."*

It's ok to ask for help, but not greedily. Don't just sit on your posterior and hog people's lifeworks because you're too lazy to build one for yourself. That's entitlement—not reward. A parasitic existence is no existence at all.

Self-reliance makes us think outside the box by igniting the blaze of ingenuity. It's acting independently and making a name for ourselves. No loopholes; no shortcuts. It unveils our divine assignments, anointed gifts, and full potential, so we can deploy what we have, earn what we get, and step meekly into the fullness of our destinies.

A self-reliant man doesn't need sophistication when push comes to shove; he just needs something that'll stick.

Melancholy or upbeat, Tatay boozed. Mum used to rebuke him for it, but he was too headstrong for her reproof. We bring levity to it by saying, the true index of a Delos Reyes is the ability to imbibe alcohol in a single bound. Years of pork rinds, Marlboros, and swills of *Tanduay,* San Miguel beer, and Ginebra rum got their deleterious hands on him—and cancer is indiscriminate.

Even for man who scraped spares to get by, Tatay needed us to lug his burdens *with* him—not for him. During the last years of his life, he'd asked others for help—by others, I meant Kuya Chris *(Kū-yā is Brother)* driving him to his chemotherapy. If Tatay felt sorry for himself or thought, *"Poor ol' me,"* he *never* showed it.

In December of 2001, he was intubated with a chest tube. Within days, his ventilator was discontinued. No hope, just a miracle in the waiting. Our family sat vigil and muttered to him, *"Lyne Lyne is coming. You have to fight."* Tatay was tired, but I needed him to stay alive, long enough for me to land in Manila, to hug him once more, to tell him, *"Thank you,"* and to say our last goodbye. A true warrior, he fought until the very end. On 12/16/2001, Tatay took his final breath—I was twenty-four hours too late.

The next time I saw Tatay was through his glass coffin.

Death had to abduct him while sleeping or he would not have succumbed.

Forever, I'm saved by his love. Tatay was larger than life, so we, too, grew strong. Everything this man promised, he proved. No man had ever fought for me the way Tatay did. It's very unlikely one ever could.

> *"If you don't know where you're from, you'll have a hard time saying where you're going."*
> - Wendell Berry

You and I are descendants of brave men—a long lineage of warriors who incurred the blowbacks. They've lobbied and lost their limbs—even laid down their lives—to facilitate our future, and promulgate the freedom and privileges we now enjoy. Our ancestors, with or without the good fortune of an upper-class edification or aristocratic heritage, had left their footprints on the sands of progress with their self-reliance, heroism, and undisputed grit. On their shoulders of legacies, we stand. Some are departed, some might've not touched us directly, but the gore of their wise counsel, self-government, and resilience surges in our veins, making us equipped and more than enough to row ourselves past uncharted waters and into the coastline of courage.

That's what courage is!

Buttressing through segregation and suffrage, disarmament

and imprisonment. Vietnam, Leyte, Shiloh, Anzio, Guam, Appomattox, and Normandy.

Courage is not *"I'm living my truth, and my fettuccine spine and cellophane skin are so offended that it's not your truth, and now, I'll use every podium until you and the world applaud my authenticity, which I'll pass off as a clarion call for social justice."*

Too crude?

> *"People say, 'You're a very tough person.' I'm not tough.. Life is tough. I'm merely trying to acquaint you to those facts."*
> - Dr. T. Sowell

These heroes took the hand they'd been dealt and sowed the seeds of self-reliance for our harvest—it's available to *anyone*. Demand it of yourself, if not of others. We've inherited their determination—not just their DNA. Among us is our forefathers' gallant spirit, to pick up the mantel of their sacrifices, and find the light in our ways—or lit that bitch up ourselves.

> *"We seem to be getting closer and closer to a situation where nobody is responsible for what they did, but we are all responsible for what someone else did."*
> - Dr. T. Sowell

What headway is made in inexhaustibly blaming the prior and/or current generation for molding you into a byproduct of a tyrannized past?

I overfed my dog; he Hershey-squirted on the furniture—blame Petco; I blew up to two hundred pounds—blame the sherbet. Blame my family, blame the ex, blame America,

Covid, the Delta variant, blame the unvaxed, the waitress who gave me wheat instead of rye, blame the ozone and the existential threat of climate change (*when did the climate ever not change?*). Blame Russia, Russia, Russia collusion. Blame the horses at the border. Blame Manny Pacquiao on the east, Ron DeSantis on the west, Rudy Giuliani up north, Alejandro Giammattei down south.

And when everything else fails, go deranged and blame a Crayola of people, starting with the bad, bad orange man, orange man bad.

> *"It's a good excuse for not getting there."*
> - Morgan Freeman
> (*My favorite actor*)

Someone, please, hand me a mirror!

Can you go through a day—half even—without blaming someone else—dead or alive—for your own improprieties?

Tatay *never* saw victimhood as a virtue—neither will I.

Progress isn't bleating about how much fighting I still have to do, but recognizing how much had already been fought.

Japanese, Chinese, and Filipino migrants drudged Hawaii's sugar plantations (*and other contributions*), but the Asian communities were among the poorest in America in the 1940's. During WWII, Asians were discriminated against, massacred, tortured, and interred in isolation camps (*you think these started with the "Chinese virus?"*). There were laws of anti-miscegenation, the Anti-Filipino riot in 1930, the Immigration Act of 1924 (*to name a few*). For Filipino WWI vets, more claims for reparation were denied than approved under the American Recovery and Reinvestment

Act of 2009. I've been called a *"Chink,"* an *"Oreo," "Not a real Filipino,"* and I've been told, *"You act white"* and *"Go back where you came from.'*

Discrimination is wrong—no matter who's doing it. Racism is wrong—no matter who's receiving it.

I *can* play that card, but I don't want it. Trigger warning: there are more enough race hustling, virtue signaling, woke wallowing, self-virtuous, yogurt brain Bolsheviks out there to do it for me. These humbugs would be irrelevant, if not jobless, if they didn't.

> *"People who don't have their own houses in order should be very careful before they go about reorganizing the world."*
> - Clinical psychologist Jordan Peterson

I don't know if the wellspring of every disparity is injustice or if all solution is infrastructure. I know racial grievances haven't stepped up to get my house in order, upturn things, or taken me to the Promised Land. I know vanguards and grassroots coalitions had barnstormed for my equal rights, and *not* equal outcome.

The outcome is incumbent on me.

A car, a house, a yacht—they're not rights, but acquisitions I *have* to earn through hard work. I don't want that epitaph on my gravestone: *"She who shrunk from life, much less did anything of any importance."*

I was a trust fund baby, disinherited by my own blood. My life won't be easy if I were to lever my father's name—like others do. It's self-reliance that pushes me to stand on my own—not to get over grievances—but to rise above them.

Why should I be socially favored above others when there is a crayon for every shade of adversity? I get there's glory in getting the alloys, but in today's Olympic oppression, you can keep the gold.

> *"From what I can learn, it was sad, certainly. But my ancestors who lived and died in it are dead. The white men who profited by their labor and lives are dead also. I have no personal memory of those times and no responsibility for them, neither has the grandson of the man who held my folks. I have no intention of wasting time beating on old graves… No, I do not weep at the world. I'm too busy sharpening my oyster knife."*
> - Anthropologist Zora Neale Hurston

As so Ms. Hurston, I live in Present-ville, where I progress instead of regress, and self-reliance goes hand in hand with responsibilities I gather with age. And not one unmoored, attention-seeking charlatan in this country or any country could convince me that I'm worse off than my uncle, my mother, my grandmother, or my great grandmother.

There's sobering freedom in knowing nobody can tell me, *"You wouldn't have that if it wasn't for me."*

Everything I have, I worked for—not on my back or down on my knees—but on my own two feet. I didn't sleep with it, marry it, or divorce it. I say this with the highest degree of humility. No hand-me-down; no gondola ride; no head start. My possessions and privileges aren't ill-gotten—and that's the hill I'd die on. I am the architect of my success; the janitor of my mess. No regrets. No apologies.

Hosting an eleventh-century, yellow, brown, Asian, self-flagellation, guilt symposium? Don't expect my RSVP.

You'll be swatted by misfortunes. Life will squash you and keep you down should you waiver. A nine to five doesn't promise financial fitness, and if overstretched, you'll learn to live with less. You can exhume the past, undercut your own strength, whine in perpetuity like a nihilistic ingrate, twerk on police cars, shriek for repayment and kickbacks, shoplift a Walgreen's up to $999 because $1 more would get you arrested (*I can't make this up*), desecrate statues, fulminate for what the world owes you, tell others to do better as you stay bitter, blame the system and institutions for making you do it—anything to misdirect the onus away from you for not getting your ducks in a row—or you can accept problems as part of life, and be your own rescue. Self-sustaining. Self-supporting. Self-reliant.

Should you need reminding of the value of committing to your own contribution:

"It is not the critic who counts; not the man who points out how the strong man stumbles, or where the doer of deeds could have done them better. The credit belongs to the man who is actually in the arena, whose face is marred by dust and sweat and blood; who strives valiantly; who errs, who comes short again and again, because there is no effort without error and shortcoming; but who does actually strive to do the deeds; who knows great enthusiasms, the great devotions; who spends himself in a worthy cause; who at the best knows in the end the triumph of high achievement, and who at the worst, if he fails, at least fails while daring greatly, so that his place shall never be with those cold and timid souls who neither know victory nor defeat."
- Theodore Roosevelt

In a world that seems to believe entitlement is everyone's birthright, I was blessed to have had self-reliance modeled for me by a man whose life is worth saluting and courage worth emulating. I give credit where credit is due: I am not starting from scratch for I was raised by a man who, even in the most fraught circumstances, remained unbowed. If Tatay, who had little to none, could make a buck, put a roof over his family's head, keep them cozy, feed, nestle, and protect them from the most inhospitable conditions, and embed the foothold for their propitious future by driving a glorified scooter, what is my excuse not to get in the arena?

Want to build back better? Make men, men again.

> *"Being deeply loved by someone gives you strength while loving someone deeply gives you courage."*
> - Lao Tzu

Tatay's love still envelops me with the strength to do the heavy lifting—even if someone else will take the credit, even if no one will remember my name, even if I have to take the blows—and loving him gives me the courage to carry the baton. He blesses me from his death, more than any man I know can, living. Since I got most, if not all, of my mordant peculiarities from him, in his way, I see my own. Tatay's words will forever carry extra weight. I still wear his favorite horseshoe amulet and hear his music and dictum: *"Speak less, work hard, stay humble."*

There isn't a day that goes by that I don't feel indebted to Tatay. He lived as he had died—a hero—my hero. He was my defender. A league above all men. In my heart and in my memory, he still is.

"For what is a man, what has he got?
If not himself, then he has naught.
To say the things he truly feels and
not the words of one who kneels.
The record shows I took the blows.
And did it
My Way."

Lyrics: P. Anka C. Francois,
J. Revaux, G. Thibaut

IN COLOR | JG GARCIA

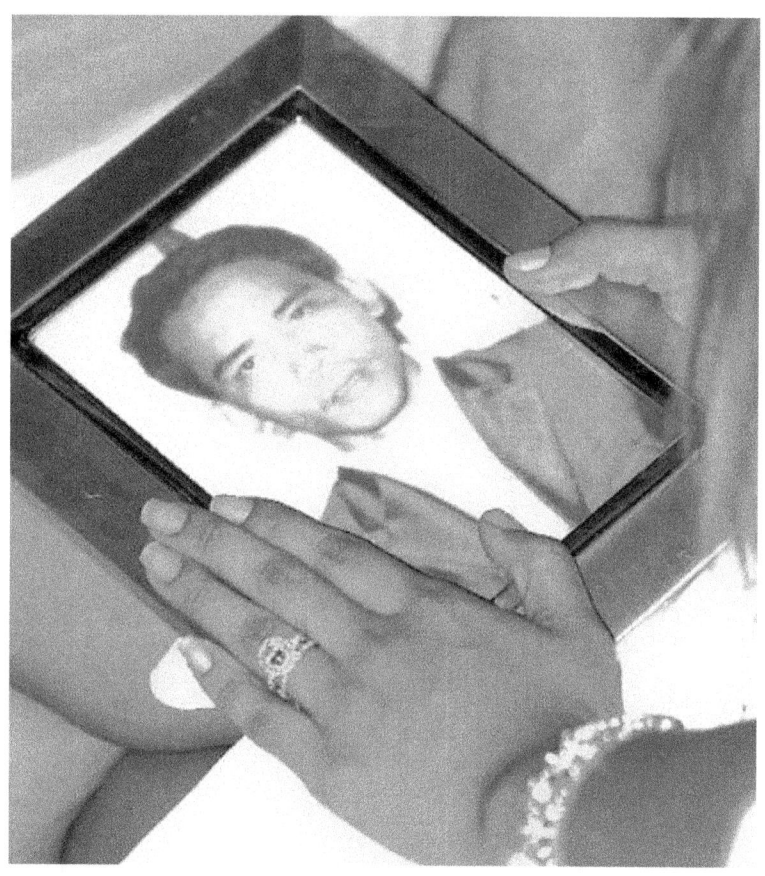

18. SAY NO TO THE DRESS

"A friend is a gift you give yourself."
- Robert Louis Stevenson

Balenciaga, Belgium truffles, jazz, Jimmy Choo, and Givenchy—my favorite things to do in D.C. with my friend Kenneth Rascher. We met in 2008 at G.W.U. hospital when he visited his friend—my patient. I was administering an antibiotic when this lad walked in and introduced himself. Bracingly handsome; I was captivated. Kenn filled the room with exhilarating energy and humor. We talked about my condo; he gave me his business card: *"KennDavid Designs."* The rest was history. The last time I was in D.C, I visited the places we loved. And a shaft of light twinkled from heaven.

My memories of Kenneth jolted me into bittersweet tears.

He was an eccentric artist, a self-proclaimed *"maximalist,"* and a designer, drawn into ombre hues and acetate textures. My dowdy, monochromatic wardrobe didn't go unnoticed as he was the mastermind behind its riveting, reupholstered, velour makeover. I still have the double-stranded, emerald, turquoise, and gold one-shoulder top, and the asymmetrical, ruffled, canary halter he picked for me thirteen years ago. Thanks in large part to Kenn's groovy sense of style, I no longer looked bedraggled. Kenn redid and reinvented my anemic wardrobe, my life—my world.

We've politely jostled over politics and spatted over the most trifling things—and flickered a table napkin on fire! He'd saved me from spin cycles of absurd decisions and held me altogether during my pre-wedding meltdown.

When my inanity was big, his love was bigger. He'd spent oodles of hours mending my heart with one hand pushing me away from playing it safe and another to catch my fall. But when it was time for me to get off the merry-go-round of boy snafus, he put his foot down.

Kenneth was driving me home when my ex-boyfriend Ben called, beseeching me to take him back.

Here's the abbreviated clip of that telenovela: In 2006, I sponsored his all-paid-for vacay from Oregon to Palo Alto, California (*where I used to live*), and he dumped me on the day he left; 2007, he cheated with a noirette, buxom in the backseat *after* I gave him another chance; 2008, I took him back, but he was so unhappy with our sexless cohabitation, he left. Now, five months later, he's calling—again…

Any question?

Kenneth knew this outlook too well. He knew I wanted to give this guy another chance—his fourth one.

"What makes Ben think he can waltz back into my life? Again! Why does he think I'll take him back this time?"

Tires screeched. Kenneth revved up his Porsche and said,

"BE—CAUSE—YOU—AL—WAYS—DO!"

"Ben keeps coming back because you can't say, 'No' to him! You're the best gal in the world, JG, but you can't see what this guy had done to you—what he keeps doing to you. It's not pretty, sweety. You've moved on. Why relapse? No, you're not calling him back. Let's go get some tarts!"

JG mystified. Did my Kenneth-baby just say *that* to me? Duly noted, Mr. Rascher.

Kenn was not a fan of Ben, so I sought a second opinion.

I took my friend Wanda out to breakfast—for sure, she'd tell me what I wanted to hear. *"No more Ben, baby girl. He breaks your heart, and we pick up the pieces."*

Strike two. Noticeably, Kenn and Wanda didn't get it.

I took my friend Virgil out to dinner—he believed in love. *"No, not Ben! I am done, done, done with you and him."*

Strike three.

I was skeptical. Did these three hatch a scheme against me and Ben at some clandestine alley? What ever happened to getting more flies with honey than with vinegar?

I had a yearlong dating hiatus after a twenty-eight-month frenzy with Ben, and I shared *everything* with Kenn about how I became the frumpy, hot mess he knew. I was stress eating from dusk to dawn, so he took me to art exhibitions, roof-top parties, cafes, and theaters, and told me to *"eat a liquid diet."* He made me laugh. He carried me through tribulations with chocolate crumpets in his hands and a halo over his head. His countenance and compassion never let up. He was my angel long before he got his wings.

I thought of all the detrimental ways to move on, but Kenn nixed them all. He knew they'd just break my heart.

"Want to break the bank instead?" he asked.

Hello Neiman Marcus!

But I was so foxed by Ben's reappearance that I wanted an encore—again. I fell into that sinkhole—again—scattered in tears, sopping in my hands—again. One weekend, Kenn taught me lessons that took me thirteen years to suss out.

"He wants to come home. I can't stop loving him, Kenn."

"No, JG! You don't have to stop loving Ben! You need to start loving yourself!"

Self-love. Boundaries. The meaning of *"No."*

It was I who didn't get it—not my well-meaning friends.

Without self-love, there's no self-respect and no boundary. With it, there's groundwork for self-evaluation and taking agency over my own life. With it, I can say, *"Yes"* to what propels me into the highest expression of myself and *"No"* to the static, interposing voices. No to events that aren't as transformative as the books I read at home; no to humdrum conversations with yahoos with IQs superseding that of a doorknob; no to being a punching bag and daring to call it love; no to crummy relationships that don't lift me higher; no to predilections that no longer fit my theology; no to propositions that are as bland as my garden burgers; and no to *"friends"* who hid when I needed help, but reemerged when it was convenient—I bade them farewell.

"Train yourself to let go of everything you fear to lose."
- Yoda

Look at your life today. Where do you want to be in five, ten, twenty years? Who's not nudging you there? What's sidetracking you? Do you find yourself unwillingly sucked back into places, patterns, and people you've outlived?

You know them. They can sniff dubiety like a bloodhound, and they know you'd give them your best with an inclusive discount (*promo code: insecure*). Hence, these dilettantes claim your time and space and befog you in saying they'd change and be better: dreaming; wishing; thinking; hoping;

planning—never doing. All bark; no bite. Rhetoric, but no results. You can schlep them off the tarmac, fill them up with motivational gasoline, buckle them in, adjust their mirrors, and vector them from the control tower, but unless they step on that gas, these laggards aren't going anywhere.

And if you wait around while they circling around the same runway, neither are you.

But you're ready for take-off, buttercup! These people are nothing but gridlocks to your growth.

If you don't typify self-love, you cannot say *"No"* to the dross that no longer further you in our destiny. Boundaries become brittle, if not absent. You and your most hallowed adytum are amenably open with a 24/7 *"Welcome"* sign. You've become your biggest issue. You invited them in! Now, you wonder why they won't leave! In other words, how you treat yourself and your space denotes the kind of treatment you'd want from others.

This is JG reporting from the Department of the Obvious.

> *"You are the first example of how people treat you."*
> - Prosperity pundit Lisa Nichols

Raise your self-love frequency; flex that *"No"* awareness muscle. For some, it'd degenerated. But you are your own border czar, and concern yourself less with fixing the root causes of why interlopers trespass on your boundaries and more on why you let them.

When Ken took me to a bridal salon, I wanted elegance and simplicity—à la Elizabeth Taylor's first dress. I wanted a lot of class—not a lot of ass! He vetoed my top three picks as he quoted Giorgio Armani: *"Elegance is not about being noticed; it's about being remembered."*

"JG, you weren't born when Liz wore that dress, yet you love it. Here's the thing—I like what you've tried on so far, but once we leave this place, I'll forget you in them."

The fourth dress—he said, *"That's the one!"* I agreed.

It was sleeveless, but showing my shoulders made me feel like a snazzy, little minx. The conical bodice was so loose, but since I'd already taken far too much of the seamstress' time, when asked if it was ok, I said, *"Yes."* Kenn stepped in, hawked, cupped my bra, and sternly said, *"Noooooo, we don't want these falling out. Make it snug, please."*

Kenneth was my lifesaver on my wedding day. He kept me sane. He got me out of my gown and squeezed me into my luau dress—no Spanx. *"You're married and naked with me!"* He always made me laugh.

Though I was one of them, Kenneth and my cleanup crew believed honesty was the best policy (*how rare these days*). They told me when I was full of it and when the turmoil was self-inflicted (*also how rare these days*). Kenn told me nothing that I've not long denied, but he did calcify these lessons on self-love. He taught me not everything in life had to be a struggle; I just insisted on making it one. Kenn taught me how to say *"No,"* how to demarcate boundaries, and how to procure what I want in life and in my personal milieu. Self-love demands no less.

Kenneth must be cheering among the angels.

He was right—I didn't have to stop loving Ben to start loving myself. When I fell in love with JG—stretch marks, muffin top, acne-prone, racoon-eyes, cellulites, flabby butt, melasma, crooked eyebrows, loopy eyelids, I-know-what-I-want-and-don't-want JG—I felt implacable, wholesome, empowered. Miranda Priestly empowered. I cemented my boundaries, spruced up the zoo I called *"mi vida,"* and undid the very persona that I and everyone who'd come to know me as: the girl who didn't love herself enough (*or at all*) to say *"No."*

Growing beyond friends and families didn't make me better than they. Whatever we had, it just ran its course. These entities didn't have to keep on waylaying my life because they didn't know what to do with theirs.

> *"If I'm in love with anybody, I'm in love with myself."*
> \- Truman Capote

Kenneth's message was pure and simple: Love yourself; the rest is easy.

There's a full gamut of ways to say *"No."* It's prickly, and it may even feel like a zero-sum powwow.

Lisa's *"Plus 3 me"* is wonderful—it leaves nobody in the hole. Don't start with *"We need to talk."* It's too ominous. Begin with *"pluses,"* then titrate:

> *"I want to tell you what I love about you (+1)*
> *what I respect about you is... (+2)*
> *what I appreciate and honor you for... (+3)*
> *What I realize is that I'm really complete with this relationship (+2)*
> *I need to love you from a distance; I just need space (+1)*
> *I need that space to begin now. (0)"*

"No" doesn't entail appendages. As Lisa said, *"No"* is a complete sentence.

VIII – YELLOW BRICK ROAD

"Out of suffering have emerged the strongest souls; the most massive characters are seared with scars."
- Khalil Gibran

19. THE MIDAS TOUCH

"Too many people spend money they earned to buy things they don't want, to impress people they don't like."
- Will Rogers

A sign that reads, *"The more you buy, the more you save"* is a stunt. Stores notoriously advertise this. Buy an item for $50 (*originally $100*), and you save 50%. On the flip side, take the bait, and you've been gaffed into spending $50. You saved nothing; you invested nothing. Potato, potah-to? Nope. Savings is tactile money stowed away—not subsidiary sediments left from spending.

If only I were an apt learner. Or this pragmatic.

I learned from financial flops—not budgetary cleverness.

I didn't gush over a 750 credit score many moons ago, but after restarting my single life, my credit skyrocketed from a number I'd rather not say to 630, and I wanted to run uphill at the Philadelphia Museum of Art with a celebratory fist and climb Everett with pyros and confetti. *Que paso?*

The reckless shopping sprees and Valentino in my twenties (*everyday was cyber Monday*), languishing health crises, the Great Recession in my thirties, the divorce, lawyer fees, inflated spousal support in my forties—it was all outflows.

"Don't save what is left after spending;
spend what is left after saving."
- Billionaire philanthropist Warren Buffet

A six-figure salary feels like a spigot of Benjamins, so it's easy to spend today's money and tomorrow's stock—until your bank account rollbacks to double digits—and you ask,

"*Where did all my money go?*" as if it walked out on its own. It's jarring to realize just how much you've misspent.

> "*A budget is telling your money where to go instead of wondering where it went.*"
> - Money maven Dave Ramsey

My *dinero* went everywhere it shouldn't had gone: I bought hundreds of posh clothing and spent thousands more on shoes to match; purchased chaffs I couldn't afford; craved stuff I didn't need; fed mouths that subsequently bit my hand; and without daily venti caramel macchiato (*my liquid Zen*), I'd have a withdrawal. I made money and lost twice as much. The divorce didn't bankrupt me, but I was well on my way. When the gale vanished, I realized money's neither good nor bad; it goes where I go. It was not the problem—I was! The stakes are lower when you're young, but I'm forty-two; I cannot just wig out irresponsibly to extravagant outlays because there's money at my disposal.

I used Dave's "*7 Baby Steps*" to fix my finances. I moved into a ratty, shoebox of an apartment and downsized in both footage and cost. *Adiós* A/C, clubhouse, doorman, outdoor pool. Without much entertainment and distraction, no Lyft, I packed lunch, bought generic, cut coupons, finetuned my priorities, scrimped, scrimped, and scrimped some more.

Frugality made me ingenious with money.

To get out of the borehole, Dave said, "*Sell so much stuff the kids think they're next!*" I don't have kids, but I've accumulated so much junk since I've moved to Hawaii that I felt owned by the things I owned! And in the early days of uncoupling, I acclimated to living alone with almost two of everything, and most were items of vacuity. With a little spatial renovation, I gave my place a facelift by tidying up and decluttering. I learned how to live with less even when it was inconvenient, value my gains, reflect on my losses, own things purposefully, and chuck the muck. Unadorned, life's serene. I spend less; I owe less. It makes meandering through life uncomplicated, and caches unspent money for rainy days. I'll take ancillary funds over insufficient ones any day of the week.

When you toss out frivolous extras in life, why cease at useless people (*I knew many*)?

Unused Tiffany & Co. cup—sold for $5. Matching $110 Pier 1 dinner trays—sold, $20. Gaudy 65-inch tv (*retailed over $5,000*) with unwrapped 3D goggles—sold for $800. As I jettisoned these materials, oddly, they felt immaterial.

> *"You've got to tell your money what to do or it will leave."*
> \- D. Ramsey

I got out of my financial funk, paid my mortgage *and* my rent, and continued to support my family without a single stimulus check or other seismic checks that made it easier to stay home. How's that for an incentive to go to work! Steadily, funds ratcheted, and I've retrieved what I've lost tenfold. It's fiscal porn! It may sound supercilious, but it's the upshot of being canny with my cash.

> *"Act your wage."*
> \- D. Ramsey

I take it down a notch. Nowadays, I run errands in lowkey ensembles: t-shirt, $10 sweatpants, $15; sneakers, $27; reclining after work in my new, midrise condo—priceless.

Can money buy happiness?

Economists and Nobel prize winners Angus Deaton and Daniel Kahneman published a study that stated money *does* buy emotional wellness, but up to a point. It doesn't make us Teflon against the untoward or excludes us from stress, but money allocates us with more options, which in turn, ameliorates our overall quality of life and satisfaction.

More than 50% of millennials think they'll be millionaires someday, over 80% of them have the ultimate goal of being wealthy, and according to an ACORN study, they spend about $3,500 a year eating out and more on coffee than on retirement plans. On average, baby boomers are more than $110,000 in debt, and Americans spend about $1,100 per year on a cup of joe.

Are these shrewd expenditures?

You tell me. How's your retirement portfolio looking? Is the economic bust of 2021 hijacking your stash of cash?

How about having the affluent *"redistribute"* their wealth?

Having them *"pay their fair share"* would've mitigated my financial hiccup, but before calling the minted *"greedy"* for keeping *their* money and debossing my ball-gown with *"Tax the rich,"* while I serve Sauvignon to the rich, eat Foie gras with the rich, and take donations from the rich, let me remind myself:

- ➢ The top 1% earns about 20% of all income in the nation.
- ➢ The top 1% pay 40% of all income tax (*twice their share of America's income*).
- ➢ The bottom 50% pays only 2.9% all income tax.

Prefer Cliff Notes? Per The American Enterprise Institute:

> *The bottom three income quintiles making up 60% of US households are net recipients—they receive more transfer payments than they pay federal taxes.*
> *The top 20% of the. households are net payer—they financing 100% of the transferred payments to the bottom 60%, and almost 100% of the collected tax revenue to run the federal government.*

In English? Enough buzzwords—the rich is already paying up the wazoo. Per taxfoundation.org:

> The top 1% pay a greater share of federal income taxes than the bottom 90% combined (*40.1% vs 28.6%*).
> The average tax rate of the top 1% is more than 7x higher than the bottom 90% combined (*25.4% vs. 4.4%*).

Too much money mumbo jumbo?

Ok, here are the facts: I was the one who borrowed a gargantuan loan for grad school. I was the one who took a scalpel through my savings with exorbitant spending. I was the one who squandered money by replacing one fashion fetish with another—Saks Fifth Avenue was my second address. I was the one who wanted to impress more than to invest. So, what's my *"fair share"* of *your* money?

Let me know—I got Venmo.

20. DO NOT DISTURB

"Myself I must remake."
- W.B. Yeats

Loneliness usually has a bad rap as indistinguishable from solitude and isolation. Research shows us that we're uncomfortable being alone without stimulus. In a University of Virginia study, two-thirds of men and a quarter of the women chose an electric shock over doing nothing and spending time alone with their thoughts. Some have anthologies of mental spam folders that unseals when we're in a solo act—myself included—we can't stand it!

Pandora's box volleys with slings and arrows, and there we are, delayed on a detour or a dead-end—alone!

What to do? We turn to and maintain *"filler friendships."*

¿Por qué? *"Because you'd rather do anything on a Friday night besides staying at home by yourself, even at the cost of spending time with people whose company you don't enjoy,"* said Filip Fröhlich of *The New York Times*.

Do you find solace in being alone? Does it petrify you?

"When people take these moments to explore their solitude, not only will they be forced to confront who they are, they just might learn a little bit about how to out-maneuver some of the toxicity that surrounds them in a social setting," said sociologist Jack Fong.

Solitude is your choice. Loneliness is a sense of seclusion you feel with or without others. Solitude is restoration. Loneliness is isolation. Socializing is being with others (*we all seem proficient at this*). Solitude is being with yourself.

"One day you will wake up and there won't be any more time to do the things you've always wanted. Do it now."
- Paulo Coelho

For me, those things are simple.

After divorce, I did bite-sized activities that rejuvenated me, not something I had to sit through with a clenched jaw: I indulged in self-care and DIY art; sat in the sun; watched the waves swooshed as I listened to the mellifluous voice of Ella Fitzgerald and Hans Zimmer's concertos; and jogged briskly with my dog. At night, I watched the last bastions of moral masculinity: *Jack Bauer* and John Wick—Keanu Reeves reruns. As a rookie writer, an avid reader, and a glue gun maniac, time alone allowed me to hone my skills until my writing gained a life of its own, go to bookshops, coffeehouses, read for leisure and didactic purpose without the uptake of mobile apps and symphonies of vibrations, and discover an invigorating influx of interests.

My newfound outlets were antibodies against aloneness. They've made the difference between joyful reflection and compulsory suffering.

Solitude has become my doorway to self-awareness—my Shangri-La.

It's my time. Don't disturb.

Did I metamorphose into a misanthropic, old lady? For a while, I did—almost agoraphobic in extremity.

Every night felt like everlasting damnation; I thought it was my penance. One minute, I'd be yowling in bed to tear-jerking ballads of Luther Vandross and then jamming in my undies to Aerosmith on full blast the next. See, balance!

Pastor Jon Burgess of the New Hope O'ahu said, *"A place of isolation turns into inspiration, dead-end turns into divine beginning, desperation turns into determination... We think it's punishment, but it's really preparation. Discontent turns into discovery."*

Do I get lonely? *Claro!*

I'd like a man to say I have a beautiful mind, not a nice ass, and razz me with a care package. An empiricist with brains to match his brawn (*without preening himself of his pecker*) and decrypt my gazes. Also an INFJ (*Myers-Briggs*) with a droll sense of humor and *Love languages* are quality time, touch, and affirmation, not gifts; he'd bring me rice cakes; talk nonstop about *The Law of Attraction*; watch *Sidewalks of New York* over quarts of diet ginger ale and pints of Cookies & Cream gelato; break away my carapace; kiss the nape of my neck; grasp the curve of my waist; purr effusive words in my ear; and share his innermost convictions. It'd be wondrous to meet an ultra-private, primped, principled man who signs the front of a check—not the back—fall in love, not be misjudged by his family until *after* they meet me (*or not at all*), have a wedding, not pay for everything (*and not have it construed as an exclusive family reunion*). walk giddily down the aisle, dance to Chantal Kreviazuk's *"Feels Like Home,"* boogie to Bruno Mars' *"Versace On The Floor,"* consummate, from my skin to his soul, on my knees, under his control, and live happily ever after.

Sounds enthralling, but after a handful of goose chases, my hope of finding "*the one*" had evaporated. Whatever iota of faith I have left in love, it won't suffice for another go.

The irony is I'm at my best when I'm alone.

Some say spinster-me just *"haven't met the right person,"* I can't bilk serendipity, and others diagnose me as *"evasive,"* *"ambivalent,"* *"scared."* There might be a tad of truth there (*sometimes I think marriage is just a forerunner; a divorce waiting to happen*), but given everything I've been through, I cannot help but be circumspect. Jesus himself resurrected from the dead just once—I don't think I can do it twice.

If by some celestial design I'd date again, it would *not* be broadcasted. I like my man incognito and our relationship offline, inside a coffer, platted on Fort Knox, girdled by a Chinese wall, and patrolled by Praetorian guards. All ya'll multimedia yentas, a sidenote: if I upload his name and/or face on any portal or syndicated column, he's not my beau.

To digress, my seventeen-month, hysteria free engagement had no litany of hand-to-chin poses, no array of minute-by-minute announcement, no countdown of all marital minutia leading up to the big day: *#isaidyes*; *#venue*; *#hishervows*; *#dreamwedding*; *#bling*; *#twodaystogo*; *#sayyestothedress*; *#marriagelicense*; *#MstoMrs*; *y*ada yada. I tied the knot in obscurity with fifteen people in attendance (*my side*), then I came to work with a wedding band and a new, hyphenated surname. *"You got married!"* they yucked at the nurses' station. To be brashly forthright, I find the gel manicure pageantries of *"OMG, right-hand-over-a-gaping-mouth-left fingers-flitting-with-diamonds"* so vapid.

This won't happen again, so take a good listen—my ex told the truth: *"My wife doesn't fire empty bullets."* Hallelujah! He got something right about me!

I am and *always* will be a fervent acolyte of soundless moves and thunderous results.

If I unload everything, what's left for me?

Back to solitude.

In a highspeed universe where 75% of doctor's visits are stress-related and burnout is a *"civilization disease,"* we could all use some *"me time."* Digitally detox. Log off. Regroup. Reframe. Replenish. Be quiet. Be still. Those with unspecified priorities, be sedentary and take control of your hierarchy—maybe then—you wouldn't be hissing so much about being *"soooooooo busy"* (*you megalomaniac*).

Solitude had been linked to self-reconfiguration, emotional regulation, creativity, and introspection. But it's not child's play. *"It might take a little bit of work before it turns into a pleasant experience,"* said Columbia University professor Matthew Bowker.

"Take the opportunity to say, 'This is the time where I can give something to myself, and just endorse that, in this moment, you are your first choice," said Dr. Thuy-vy Nguyen of Durham University.

Can it get better than that? You, being your first choice?

Solitude is the most straightforward passage to peace. It has one requisite: yourself.

21. THANK HEAVEN

"Gratitude is not only the greatest of virtues but the parent of all others rising."
- Marcus Tullius Cicero

Indonesia's tourist hub is Bali; Denpasar is the capital. If Philippines and Hawaii had a baby, to my eyes, it'd bear a resemblance to Denpasar—my cabalistic wicket and eastern mecca where respite, openness, firmament, and divinity meet. My first trip to Bali was in 2017, and it left a strong impression on me that over the next four years, I've sojourned to Bali every year thereafter (*pre-pandemic*). As I'm writing this book, I'm planning my fourth return.

I'm grateful for travel.

A change in geography is an expansion of viewpoint and an exploration of oneself. It's a joyride that stops the control freak in me from slaving away at itineraries and to-do list and just unwind. It used to take an act of Congress for me to power down, unplug, and unblock, but these days—even without a spa visit—it's easier to decompress. There at the southern seaboard of Bali, I learned to lunge into stillness with less defiance to receive in ways I haven't before.

Bali is vibrant, tonic, and lush. Its burgs are unpretentious; life is modest—so is the population. I'd never seen a place quite like it where even the most quotidian acts of praying and breathing seem whimsical and involute. Offerings and festivals occur like clockwork. Somewhere among the lore, museums, rice terraces, palaces, and temples is a construct of a supreme atman they call Yahweh, Jehovah, Elohim, Allah, or Krishna. If I must give it a name, I call it *"God."*

It has a stronghold in me—even more vivacious in Bali.

There are *warungs* for the foodies and (*crazy*) Kuta for post 2 a.m. horseplay. Spend days of inertia along the unpaved beachfronts of Canggu or feel a resurgence of energy from its hippie hotspots. And for the optimum digital sabbatical, be present in contentment without a cognitive load with an Ayurvedic massage or in an ashram in Ubud.

It's indubitable —I'm happiest and most alive in Bali.

Once I read, *"Feed your soul, starve your ego."*

With the very ethereal facet that makes Bali—well, Bali—how could you not do both? Isn't it the verdant oasis where legions of hedonistic seekers with strained relationships or on the heaps of midlife conundrums swarm for revelation and epiphany?

I found such hints from heaven before I left Bali in 2017. I also took with me another blessing: a new friendship.

Setia was my tour guide, turned friend, turned brother. We met when his wife was pregnant with their first baby, and now, they have their second. Setia's delightfully silly and a real hoot (*how do you think I learned the local lingo?* My family and I are so fond of him—we feel he's *ohana*. His kindness and generosity cut across cultural lines. Setia's a hard worker and a believer of *Tuhan*. His service is more than an excursion; it's a magnificent peek at his culture and its richness—given with gusto and love. Most of what I know and appreciate about Bali, I've learned from him.

In 2018, Mum turned 69, and I returned to Bali with her and my epicurean sister Marian. From the valet to our butler, The Ritz Carlton staff was stupendous.

IN COLOR | JG GARCIA

*Lempuyang Temple avec Mademoiselle Nikki Mabitazan.
Aku Cinta Kamu, Bali! Matur Suksma, Setia!*

Our suite was festooned with garlands and balloons, and we were overindulged with complimentary macaroons, Frasier cakes, exotic fruits, chocolates, and bottomless drinks. And a monkey nabbed Marian's glasses at Uluwatu!

The following year, Marian's daughter Nikki (*my mini-me niece*) and I cannonballed through Bali until we conked out. Nikki puckered and posed at Mad Pods, sashayed down Tukad Cepung waterfall and Besakih temple, and flounced around the Lempuyang Temple while Setia and I imitated her on the side with our daft jokes. We found Nemo while sea walking in Nusa Dua, chowed down acaí bowls at The Kynd, brunched at Corner House in Seminyak, and gave praise in the holy water of Tirta Empul temple—built circa 960 AD. Legend says God Indra pierced this ground and purified and cured his fallen brigade with the spurted water. These are times we cherish...

And that speakeasy bar on Petitenget Street with the best connoisseurs and a French Louis XV style armchair in the back—I want another night with you...

I'm grateful for my trip to India with Mum and Marian. With the foods, art, architecture, and amiability, our bellies and hearts were full. Sis loves spices, and turmeric makes her taste buds twirl, so her palate rejoiced in New Delhi. While at India Gate, I learned she's rapt with transnational history and monolithic buildings. My bucket list checked: Raj Gat—a memorial to the venerable Mahatma Gandhi. His cremation spot was made out of black marble—topped with an eternal flame. We had to walk barefoot around it. With the sweltering heat, our feet blistered within seconds.

The World Wonders—three down, four to go...

I've spent months physically and mentally priming for the Great Wall of China. Then detours: I wasn't cleared to fly due to a debilitating condition; and I needed I.V. infusions twice weekly.

I'm grateful for the corrective measures of medicine.

Living with disabilities, I'm grateful I can still write while hooked to a pole, thanks to my team of doctors, nurses, and ancillary personnel. My heart rate is irregular, but my heart is elastic—gratitude is the grit that reanimates it.

On September 4, 2020, guided by trust and thankfulness, I made it to The Great Wall. People outpaced me, but I ran my own race—to my own rhythm and cadence. The steps were rugged, the elevation, strenuous (*an ambulance was stationed by the entrance, pro re nata*). Reaching my point took two hours. I sat, hydrated, and rested—I didn't quit.

After convalescing, I signed up for my first American Heart Association walk. Again, I was prodromal and sluggish, and people outwent me, but with Metoprolol, Albuterol, and a portable oximeter, I made it—no quitting!

I'm grateful for my health.

My resting heart rate is 160. I went into metabolic acidosis from doing keto and came gnarly close to meeting St. Peter. Angina, vertigo, dyspnea, and dysautonomia get me cooped up for days—even weeks. Hypoglycemia comes and goes. Nausea from gastroparesis spoils my appetite. I had a right elbow arthroscopy due to osteochondritis dissecans. Left-hand dystonia, polycystic kidneys and liver, and black-outs in an elevator, in a grocery store, and on a patient's bed.

In short, I'm medically screwed up.

Our bodies keep score of every dejection, every dagger, every aftershock. Don't wait until it shuts down before you slow down. Given my profession, you'd think I know this.

My 5'1 body carted 170 pounds of emotional, physical, and mental litter—until it no longer could. There on the other side of a stretcher, it registered: make time for wellness or make time for illness. A lesson that came with ketonuria, swollen ankles, and a 6.9 blood pH *(<7 can be fatal)*, but it was a lesson, nonetheless.

All that evolved in the last few years created emotions and health commotions I didn't foresee, but with the help of a friend, I ferreted out strength I didn't know I had.

My friend Spencer—a trainer and artist dynamite—rewired and helped me see past the vanity of looking slim in a size 2. There wasn't an armor that Spencer didn't disassemble at some point of my training—by a light touch or a mental bulldozer. Rest was ok, but only with the "*3 Ps*": pass out; puke; poop—not pain. Once Spencer told me to push him with everything I got while enunciating, *"I'm a warrior."* JG Lite mumbled; Spencer didn't move an inch. He made me push, and push, and push, and repeat those words until they rumbled from my chest cavity and weaved themselves into every fiber of my being.

Shedding 60 pounds with a bad ticker that was not to beat greater than 130/minute was grueling and glacial, but with calisthenics of proportional nutrition, radical restraint, and self-discipline, I got my groove back. JG 2.0. Beast mode!

When your spirit's petering out, when you think you have no fight left in you, here's the song Spencer played for me at the end of my training. Let it reignite you…

*"I put my armor on, show you how strong I am. I put my armor on. I'll show you that I am **UNSTOPPABLE**. I'm a Porsche with no brakes. I'm invincible. Yeah, I win every single game. I'm so powerful. I don't need batteries to play. I'm so confident. Yeah, I'm **UNSTOPPABLE** today." - Sia*

I'm grateful for my family.

According to Forbes, about 95 million diurnal images are posted on Instagram, 500 tweets are sent, and 400 hours of YouTube videos are vodcasted. A 2017 study reported 36 subjects took more than 8 selfies a day, and Android users took 93 million daily selfies in 2019. Having smartphones on our desks decreases work memory by 10%, and per a Microsoft study, attention span had plummeted from 12 seconds in 2000 to 8.25 seconds in 2015. A goldfish has a longer attention span of 9 seconds.

Have we gotten dumber with our *"smart"* gadgets? Do we fill our downtime compulsively fiddling on our phones and scrolling for incoming approval indicia such as *"tags"* and *"likes"* that we don't have time left for family?

Speaking of, my family is the linchpin to my sanity—my soul sustenance. I'm grateful for them. Most live overseas, but we've vogaged together, making our *ohana* time even more pivotal and me less homesick. Our quirkiness, lunacy, love—and squabbles—make us indivisible. They've hefted me whenever I was run-down. When branches of ourselves break off, in the thick of things, we have each other and *"Karma, Karma, Karma, Karma"* chameleon karaoke!

Words fail me when I ponder the profusion of blessings I've received after all I've lost. In the last four years, I've been published, I've visited three neighboring islands, eight states, and five countries, and I got a Bichon Frisé cotton ball who licks me until kingdom come. I'm overjoyed as a caged door opened and unearthed my freedom. It may not be much, but I feel like a phoenix rising.

My blessings are both what I've been given and denied.

What more?

Call me a neanderthal, but I'm grateful to be an American. I'm inordinately lucky to live indoor, with electricity and plumbing, in a liberty-loving country where I can practice my faith without being sent to an abattoir, leave my house without a man's permission, and have access to academia, medical care, and a plethora of opportunities that sustain my my staples, but I often take for granted. I'm old enough to remember living in the Philippines, my birthland, under its Martial Law, authoritarianism, corruption, infrastructure extravagance, unrest, inflation, *"People Power"* revolution. Universities, speech, media—usurped. Where I came from, a dictator is feared—not mocked during comedy hour or scorned at every given chance. *"Activist"*? *"Safe space"*? Whistleblowers? Fake news? Try them—and you'll know what extrajudicial killing is—you can forget your fourth, fifth, sixth amendment rights. The U.S. is going someplace that looks very much like where I'd been, but having lived on both sides of the Atlantic makes me more appreciative of its tolerance, generosity, decency. Not perfect, but what country is? *"Even those who say they hate this country refuse to leave,"* said Charlie Kirk of Turning Point USA. I'll castigate America for not living up to its highest ideals when I live up to mine. If it were a cesspool of bigotry and hatred, I don't know why more than 40,000,000 immigrants had fled to it—not from it. I'm grateful for the freedom to say I love this land—the very freedom exercised by others to say they don't. If they think this counrty is so wicked, they should get a passport, find a better one, and stay there.

Who needs outside jihadist threats when we—Americans—are disintegrating each other here at home?

I'm grateful for the sacrifice and service of U.S. military.

I stand for its flag, and to my knees, I fall for its Creator. Though I haven't always been good to her, and I don't have the privileges of a 24-four hour, taxpayer funded security, a Martha's Vineyard, Montecito, Beverly Hills, Bel-Air, and Maui mansions, mega-million books and Netflix deals, and the helicopters, housekeepers, chauffeurs, fame, and power of a standout celeb, America has been good to me. But if *that* life is Jim Crow 2.0, sign me up!

I'm grateful for Hawaii's bus drivers. I'm grateful for the Honolulu Police Department who protected me from the person who *"was going to kill [me]."*

For each benison I appreciate, more favors follow—and I feel more grateful now than any other time in the last four decades. Much obliged; much to look forward to.

> *"Feeling gratitude and not expressing it is like wrapping a present and not giving it."*
> - William Arthur Ward

What do I love more than Jacqueline Oanasis Kennedy's poise and pearls? Her written *Thank You* notes! Try them! Much like her sartorial glamour, gratitude is ageless—it'll never go out of style. It augments the things you treasure.

Gratitude is the yellow brick road.

Harvard Health Publishing wrote, *"Gratitude is a way for people to appreciate what they have instead of always reaching for something in the hopes it will make them happier, or thinking they can't feel satisfied until every physical and material need is met. Gratitude helps people refocus on what they have instead of what they lack."*

Ingratitude—accompanied by resentment and anger—is the most mephitic of all human traits. I've never met a happy, ungrateful person. Have you?

Gratitude's snowball effects had been linked to better sleep and better health (*who doesn't want better sleep?*).

You can journal, meditate, or pray your way into stronger immunity and gratefulness. Don't wait for a turkey to be thankful—pay homage to your harvest now. When you do, think of those eeking out on a fraction of what you have and how desirous you'd be if you didn't have them.

22. FUREVER

"Everything I know I learned from dogs."
- Nora Roberts

July 4, 2018. The date God brought heaven down—it felt like Christmas in the summer. Independence Day came with a bang for a miscellany of reasons. On that day, my attitude towards the savagery and suffering of dogs had a wider orbit—it expanded towards *all* animals. Every year, over 6 million animals are taken into shelters, about 1.5 million are euthanized, and 71 million pet cats and 70 million pet dogs are assaulted per minute. Do you know 75% of viral diseases are caused by animal exploitation? Dogs are used for Iditarod sledding in artic weather, then butchered when no longer in need. Metal rods are rammed up the spines of crocodiles for premier purses, and animals are electrocuted, mutilated, skinned, branded, and boiled *alive* for leather, sweaters, angora, wool, milk, sportswear, and make-up testing. From animal immolating to bestiality to culling, I had a wake-up call.

All my life, I've searched for someone to come home to, fill my world with glee, glue me together, steal my heart, make it go pitter-patter, and not give it back. Someone who'd curl up me all day, unfazed. *Gracias a Dios*, I've found him! And life rushed back in. One look into his perky ears and button-round eyes, and I'm spellbound. His love and loyalty are incomparable with everything I used to know. He's a barrel of mirth and animation. Intelligent. Titanic temperament. Protective. Impish. And here's a first—the icing on the cake—when I took him home, he became my mother's favorite.

Here he is (*on his third birthday*)! My rebel with paws, Velcro baby, walking buddy, Butterball, buddha, therapist, human doorbell, and the purest love I know—James Dean! Named after Hollywood's quintessential maverick.

J.D. has been featured in Island Dog Magazine. From Mō'ili'ili to Makiki, a paparazzi of dog lovers queues to take pictures of and with my furball! This bonnie Bichon has raincoats, neckties, bathrobes, bookbags—you name it!

I thought I was ill-fitted to care for anything bigger than I. I thought the lookout for love was as doleful as love itself. I thought nobody gave without the expectation of return. I thought the world was a hellfire of unfounded truth and misplaced loyalty, and all that's ingenuous and pure was a figment of my imagination. And then I met James Dean!

Because of my J.D., consuming anything with a mother is against my constitution—and it comes with health benefits.

If you don't believe anything I say, believe this: animals do *not* offer their milk, skin, fur, babies, or themselves to be in dogfights or be tested, eaten, ridden, or worn. *Nothing* is festive about the annual *Yulin Dog Meat Festival* or the inhumane scalping and beatings of elephants to get them to lumber down a river in Thailand while carrying your ass. Think of *how* animals make their way to your plates from slaughterhouses and to those "*sanctuaries*" from wildlife.

It's outright heartless and barbaric.

> *"Dogs do know how comfortable you are with yourself, how happy you are, how fearful you are, and what is missing inside of you."*
> - From the church of Cesar Millan

My pooch monitors me whenever I take a whiz, nibbles at my hairclips, makes the most plink sound when begging for treats, rustles the papers on my desk—then pees on them—but when he smooches me with googly eyes, and I see his plumed, bushy tail flutter, I'm unafraid to love back. "*A man's best friend*" isn't an aphorism anymore—it's reality. It's a world I might've otherwise not discovered, had his love—one without motives or limits—not pulled me from the ledge. I know what's real, honest, and beautiful when I look at him. I'm homing in on being a better fur Mum and a better person because of my Pavlovian prince, my Simba against intruders, my fountain of youth, my felicity, and the greatest thing that ever happened to me. He's perfection—or as close to it I've ever seen.

I couldn't love you more, James Dean.

23. GOLIATH

"You've seen my descent, now watch my rising."
- Rumi

Gray flecks of dust overlaid the benches of the Taj Mahal—the iconic forty-two-acre mausoleum on the southern banks of the Yamuna River in Agra, India. In 1631, Mughal emperor Shah Jahan commissioned this seventeenth-century complex to immortalize his second wife—the mother of his fourteen children—his consort, and beloved Empress Mumtaz Mahal. She died from childbirth that same year. Provisions were imported from Asia, and over twenty thousand craftsmen from the Ottoman empire, Persia, Europe, and India were employed (*costed about ₹32 million rupees*). In 1963, the monument was completed.

The main gateway, capped by umbrella cupolas, are made of red Sikri sandstone. The pavilion entrance are inscribed with onyx Quranic verses. In front is the Charbagh garden, enwreathed with crenellated walls and bedecked with trees, fountains, and flowerbeds, bilaterally furcated in the middle by watercourses and walkways. The Ornamental pool to the east, the mosque facing the tomb, to the west. Resting on a seven-meter tall plinth to the north, flanked by a shedload of decorative spires and four slender minarets, below four identical kiosks, and crowned with an inverted lotus, is the palatial onion dome, built with white Makrana marbles—its apex, two hundred forty feet. Pass the *pishtaq* and recessed archways framing the incrusted balustrades and corrugated cornices is its chamfered interior chamber—garnished with semi-precious stones. Dados, paneled with foliage motifs, are below the spandrels, embossed with Arabic calligraphy.

Lurid counters are etched with pearly vines, and pigmented surfaces glare against the snowy inlays. Baroque pathways are saturated with incarnadine tiles to contrast the painted shades of its exterior elements and accentuate its geometric patterns. Surmounting the octagonal cenotaph of Mumtaz Mahal is a vaulted ceiling; her real sarcophagus is below the hall, in the lower crypt—entombing her actual remains.

In 1658, her third son Aurangzeb deposed and incarcerated his father. Ailing, woeful, and dethroned by his own flesh, Shah Jahan was kept under house arrest at a fort across the shrine he actuated for his wife, until his death in 1666. His grave is adjacent to Mumtaz Mahal.

Today and beyond, the Taj Mahal glistens in the annals of architecture. It's one of the Seven Wonders of the world, a colossus masterpiece, styled with finesse and intricacies, a fluid amalgamation of Persian, Indian, and Islamic culture, a UNESCO World Heritage site, a personification of love and grandeur, and a melded unison of sapphires, amethysts, rubies, cornelians, jades, and garnets.

Iridescent carved paintings, perforated lattices, and *pietra dura* intensify its luminosity, and yet its reflection on the central basin is always unchanged—its luster ablaze.

Over the years, militant bombardments, vehicular exhaust, air pollution, oxidation, rain, and other nearby emissions had lurked over the preservation efforts of this compound, but with its steel inception, it's uneroded. The Taj Mahal is radiant at any given time—breathtaking and illuminating. Gloam from the crescent moon can't subdue its splendor; shadows from the sun can't eclipse its glimmer. It can't be overshadowed. A paragon of symmetry, balance, harmony.

Its ivory composition wasn't only hewed with practicality; its patchwork was created with a purpose.

The Taj Mahal is a totem of blood and betrayal, tribute and trials, love and loss. It outlasts the test of time.

It's a mosaic of aesthetically broken pieces.

Its story lives within humanity—within you and me.

As a youngster, I planned to be a slam dunk success. I was the poster child of diligent schooling, galas and obedience, the benchmark of an exemplary existence, and the girl who had it all—from the boardwalk to the boardroom. The right universities, the right burgher, the right dress size, the right career, the right man.

Apparently, I was asymptomatic. All was black and white.

But nothing was what it seemed. Nothing.

The psychiatry of my past had shuddered me to my decline as much as it'd perched me to success. Pizazz and plaques camouflaged years of inferno, too macabre to recount, too grotesque to stomach. Born out of wedlock, my childhood wasn't cartwheels and cartoons. Incest had stolen my prior state of innocence and taunted me into catatonia. As I got older—beaten and blue—I saw the worst of human nature. I took a pounding from every aspect of abuse, locked horns with violence, got chewed off, knocked down, kicked out.

On the surface—in the minds of many—I'd won in all areas of life—my magnetic life. But beneath the bravado, I was sleepwalking through traumas. Denial was my drug of choice for a life so vacuous, so warped, it bears negligible similarity to the reclaimed one I now call my own.

I knew the drill, the algorithm, the deadline: accede to the rules of those whose primordial beliefs I dared not disavow and demands I dared not decry; take the vows of chastity; attend a prestigious university; make conventional choices; find a rakish Nobel Laureate with loafers and a briefcase or a chino and cardigan bedizen, Fulbright scholar; Syrah at Nobu; soirée at The Carlyle; be a virginal wife by twenty, thirty the latest; and a cobblestone house with chandeliers.

To their delight, I was obsequious to cultural conditioning. If I achieved *their* milestones, I'd be at the highest echelon, untouched by everything unkind—or so I thought.

All the while—underneath the gruff exterior and behind the smiles—was a girl shackled to secrets and shame, unwell and gaunt, forlorn and fray—surviving—but praying every breath to be her last and waiting to be rescued. But the pain didn't subside.

The cavalry never came.

By forty-three, I'd lived a life only a few could imagine—on abounding altitudes—and yet recurrently, I've attempted to take my own.

Urging for love outside my laurels, I turned to marriage. I forecasted its ending before its onset. It was a travesty and a mistake—my punishment was to stay in it. After a six-year ruse—disinclined to continue living under a deception that dissimulated itself as a daydream—I left my husband. And everything I knew, and all that was comfortable, strew with the unraveling of my marriage. I've tottered around demolition years before I wed, so divorce tripped the wire.

It was the final straw. I was a body bag.

In hindsight, I was at the epicenter of all my afflictions. I did the handiwork of all my fiascos. I'm the culmination of the decisions I made and those I aborted. Operating out of unconsciousness, I circumvented the same excuses, same lies, same people—and kept redefining rock bottom.

Nothing more to do, but start again. But this time, turn the page and turn within for a plunge into self-awareness and self-mastery. No fast-tracked fixes; no made-do penitent.

Unshakeable and invincible, I reckoned the only person I'm destined to become is the one I chose to be.

Up until those direful days of divorce, I was Herculean—deluded in feeling impregnable. I had to be the last woman standing. Arrogantly stoked by accolades, I savored in my strengths—not receptive or aware of the one rudimentary component of my being: my shadow. That wasn't self-awareness—not remotely near its vicinity.

Four years ago, I sat across someone outside a liquor store in Bali, spit balling about my kaput marriage and pending divorce. He lit up a cigarette and cued me to blather on. This unattached man could befriend any Balinese woman with his mesmerizing demeanor.

Why was he harking to a yakking harebrain?

I asked him.

"Why are you here with me, listening to my problems? You're on vacation! You should be out, meeting girls!"

I inhaled the updraft of smoke that wafted from his lips to mine, and he replied, *"I want to get to know you."*

I didn't have the foggiest idea who I was then, but what I'd give to go back to that night—now that I know who I am.

Unlike that unforgettable night, my circuitous journey to self-discovery and self-awareness was neither seamless nor ecstatic. It was an odyssey of umpteen speedbumps, and a rowdy route that didn't collude with self-preservation.

If it doesn't unnerve your ego, it's not self-awareness. If it doesn't feel like a needle in the arm, it's not self-awareness. If it doesn't unhook that chip off your shoulder or convulse and stump you into disarray, it's not self-awareness. If you aren't hurled into a whirlwind, yanked from the shallow, or you don't feel waterboarded by your own shadow, it's not self-awareness.

Having watched *King Kong* too many times, I asked my Taj Mahal guide what would happen if one—if not four—of the minarets, were to tumble down, with each being one hundred and thirty feet tall. That'd be a megaton of rocks pulverizing both the ossuaries of Mumtaz Mahal and Shah Jahan. He said the minarets were set up somewhat outside the plinth, so should any or all implode, they'd do so away from the focal point—and the burials would be unharmed. He said the carpenters knew what they were working with.

I couldn't say the same about me.

I could quote Aristotle, but if I don't scrutinize my own dimness, I'd still be a dupe. I could furbish my craven moral compass with as much fanfare on Twitter, but if I don't tussle with my own turpitude, I'd still be morally decayed. I've used a medley of non-pharmacological and medicinal analgesics, trying to anesthetize my shadow, but its maw kept gnawing at me until I—like it or not—realized what I said about others was my understanding of myself. The faults I saw in them were my own, and the one person worse than those who maltreated and dejected me was me. Because I let them. They gorged on my weaknesses while I overestimated my strengths.

My minarets were misaligned.

The two cornerstones of my writing: self-awareness is one. There is no paucity of tenuous slogans, so with this book, I feel morally impelled to hold up the mirror and adjure you to go to the deep end. Your shadow will discombobulate you, maul you like a wrecking ball, chomp you with a ton of bricks, then rub salt on your wound—until it has your undivided attention. When it's meshed in with your light, it'll cradle you like a blankie.

You've integrated.

If I beam the limelight on everything but self-awareness, this book's botched.

A shadow is a blockage of light, so by that coherence, it's a waymark towards that direction—towards the light. If you gracefully fuse this duality, for transformation, there'll be no sanctimony to aggrandize you and no timidity for others to exploit. There'll be wholeness and equilibrium.

This is when the party begins.

With self-awareness, I stopped skewering others for the very things I did myself. I realized my inferiorities weren't outgrowths of another's superiority. I still have work to do, but with self-awareness and an internal locus of control, I buckle up better during ruckuses, I care little about being unliked, and less reactive to rubbish. I'm done calibrating my settings to fit every man's screen. I'm done explaining myself. I'm done shrinking and puffing to accommodate anyone's crate. I have nothing to prove; no one to please. I know me. Those who don't know me don't deserve to.

Best of all, I'm done snubbing my shadow while letting a boy live in it.

My *amiga* Amanda habitually asks: *"Where's Mr. Right?" "When will it all end?"* and *"Why me?"* Newsflash: I ain't Google. I love this *"hookah,"* but her questions are right up there with *"Will there be a climate change apocalypse in 2030?"* They're inexplicably lousy. They're for later. Now is all we have. When embroiled in bewilderment, nowhere else to turn, nothing more to give, and nothing left to lose, the answers are always much closer to home.

Let me douse the suspense with what I do know: you get more from where you put your focus; the goalpost will be moved by chance, karma, or/and scientists; you've outlived 100% of your past, every fumble, every blooper; and with life in flux, you'll go through more changes. Count on it.

Scaffoldings encircled the Taj Mahal in 1942, 1965, and 1971 when targeted by the Japanese Air Force and bomber pilots of the Indo-Pakistan wars. It was foreseen to crater by 2016. But it's still standing. I guess steadfast greatness is minacious to those who haven't owned their gloom.

Enters resilience.

As you stride to the apotheosis of your story, those in the slump will want nothing more than to hoist themselves by undermining you. Naysayers will enervate you; hordes of haters will harry you. Negativity will do you in; trepidation will hold you back. Friends are no exception—those who will renege on their words. You might've laid your life for them, but they won't vouch for you now. When you clinch that torch, they'll railroad you and try to wrest it away, with Jedi mind tricks that it won't be done—it can't be done. Slain, you'll believe your fate to be a faulty life: a passable career; a lackluster marriage; systemic monstrosities; and half-ass healing. They'll mangle you with maliciousness, then harpoon your rib to reassure you are indeed impaled.

What now, soldier?

You're at an impasse—deserted at the bottom of the ninth. You have no mental pillar left in the tank. You've lost it all; you've given your all. No friends or lovers in lockstep. Vacillating, you want to wave the white flag.

Roger that.

Here's the kink in the story: athletes had slacked by double digits; and heavyweights had been sucker-punched. Still, they levitate like dynamo southpaws—and so will you.

You're far from definitive. You're unfinished.

Torrents of adversities might've brought you to your knees because you're human, but you're not giving up because you're valiant. Take your bludgeoned ass back in the ring, marshal whatever ounce of gall you have left, and lob your projectiles down the bore until you wear out the riffling. Waddle your weary self to the twelfth round—don't throw in the towel. Grunt your way to the fourth quarter—don't you concede. At the one-yard line, although bogged down, character—not caliber—will hasten you to the endzone.

"*Rudy*" Ruettiger was "*too small*"; Vince Papale "*too old.*" Tom Brady, "*just about done.*" That undersized dyslexic was carried off the Notre Dame field. That thirty-year-old rookie caught a pass at the forty-nine-yard touchdown. And that forty-four-year-old was Super Bowl LV MVP; his seventh win. These champs have bulletproof perseverance. They have the heart of an underdog.

So do you, and I'm rooting for you.

If they outrun, outsmart, or outperform you, shake it off. The consequences of your efforts and choices have very little to do with which armistices are being brokered by the

Black sea or who's sitting or not sitting on the White House and a lot more with whether you're the adult in *your* room, and who you see in the mirror. There is your most durable weapon and singular competition. Learn the scope of your potentials, and make each day a progression from the last.

> *"Authentic happiness derives from raising the bar for yourself, not rating yourself against others."*
> - Dr. Martin Seligman
> Pioneer of resilience and Positive Psychology

I was a lass, raised in a poky, shotgun, Philippine hovel; I was late talker (*Mum thought I was retarded*), disowned, aggrieved, and molested. I wasn't supposed to flourish, but I did. I've slept on dormitory desks and munched on ration from public housing and unconsumed slops from canteens. I wasn't supposed to finish college, but I did.

My teacher told me I couldn't write a sentence. I wasn't supposed to author a book, but I did.

Tainted by the opprobrium of divorce, I thought I could never love again—but did—that's twice more than some.

But the right person isn't always contemporaneous with the right time—it's life's most heartbreaking prank.

And what I feel for him runs deeper than the undertow of the seen and unseen. It'll never be, but it was worthwhile.

Living in his memories, of which I have many, I realized he was far easier to love than he was to hate. He'd shown me a place where words weren't needed, good triumphed over evil, and a girl like me could hope for a better life—even for a man like him. His words, I'll always remember; his face, I'll never forget. If his last words were a promise, I took it as one. He knew more about me than he thought. My safe haven, though never my lover or my friend. Truth and warmth were palpable, and I understood what sonnets were and what troubadours wrote about. In a constellation where there's a god without judgment, a world without sin, people without masks, and consciousness without guilt, he could take me there again, and the future would be waiting. But Bali was all we had—our one-time tryst with destiny. A glimpse of what might've been. This was *not* my desired outcome, but anything less would've been inconsequential; anything more, impossible. Whatever's left unspoken, I've said on these pages. Try as I may, I cannot squelch what's inside for he's as much a part of me as the air I breathe; his hold on my heart transcends through this lifespan and into the next. But who's to know where we'll be? There's not a day that I don't think of him. Even now, all that I am after him is more beautiful than before. Even now, I still feel him from afar. Even now, I dearly miss him. Even now...

This is the journey that'd brought me here, and it's been a ginormous Gordian knot. I've been a wife, a waif, a friend, a foe. I've known every inch of isolation, and I've seen the obverse side of that same abandonment coin. I've paid a steep price for fragmenting myself to make others whole. I've turned nothings into somethings. I've had it all, then gone in reverse. I've been tackled so far outside my values that in one fell swoop, I've destroyed what little I had left. I've succeeded and failed in equal measure. I've checked off the boxes of a life well-lived because winning was the name of the game.

I've donned on countless masks that I didn't know where my false identity ended and where my true self began.

But it is what it is. If you've extrapolated nothing from my stories by now, know this: I've fallen ninety-nine times, got up a hundred.

I've done nothing worthy of the Congressional Medal, but under these circumstance, I've done my best as well as best could be. A day will come when I'm not the agile dame I am now, but in my own right, I am—and will be always—the heroine of my story. Not can, not may, but will. That's a victory in and of itself.

> *"I am not what happened to me,*
> *I am what I choose to become."*
> *- Carl Jung*

Christ didn't refuse the cross; He knows what I can bear. I'll carry my own for what are friendship, loyalty, courage, love, trust, faith, strength, patience, and resilience if they cannot withstand the test?

Occasionally, life throws a wrench into my plans—undoing all I've done, and I pout, and Hail Mary my way through another nightfall. But life is just as jaded staying leaden as it is mulling over what could've been, so I chose rebirth from ruins—to live until I expire. I chose to love someone I couldn't have and let go of the one I had, but couldn't love. For all I care, what's gone can stay gone. I accept who I've been, and I love who I'm becoming. I'm my accountability's only constituent. My breakthrough isn't for anyone. My come-back is for me.

I pray that when faced with my brothers and sisters here and the gatekeepers of the afterlife that who I am/was will be more important than what I look(*ed*) like, that I'll be judged—not how I was born—but how I've behaved, not based on my genitals, but if I've done any good, not how much melanin I had, but if had any morals at all, and if I did what I said I'd do. May I be loved or hated, punished or pardoned, a disapproved heretic or a favored hero—not for what my tribal clique deserves—but for what I—the individual—deserve.

May I not be pegged as an Asian, heterosexual, vaccinated, cisgender, middle-class, Catholic, divorced, conservative, disabled woman, but be remembered only as a person, and a child of God. No cosmetics.

At the behest of the Most High, I wholeheartedly entrust my life into His hands and lay my all at His feet—kneeling only to the One who died for my sins. He's my lifeline and my one set of footprints. When God created me, He made no mistake.

From the sprawling metropolis of the Philippines to Silicon Valley, from the madness to the mountaintop, I've learned this immutable truth:

> *"I am the vine, you are the branches. He who abides in Me, and I in him, bears much fruit; for without Me you can do nothing."*
> - John 15:5

I've only just begun to listen and understand, and so until the Grandmaster rings that bell, it's forward march.

All aboard?

If you're hanging by a thread, with all that is homely and safe strewn under emotional fatigue, raging times will test your every finitude—down to your last crumbs of courage. They'll galvanize you into concrete actions because doing is the only option—talking is not. You don't need a badge, credential, or trophy to get the hurrah. Shift in both habits and mindset, rise above the prepackaged excuses, and soar for the betterment of your family, church, community, and country. Roar to those who'd placed their bets against you, wanting to see you fail.

You could cure cancer, and these prats will still twine, *"What about diabetes?"*

Nothing will ever be enough for those who pursue hate—not happiness.

And foremost, do it for you—for the manifestation of your best self and the plowing of your abundance.

In pursuant to the masonry of your own Taj Mahal and its stonewall, reaffirm to yourself that though you won't have a dearth of mistakes—unheeded or repeated—you're an emblem of resilience. You're adequate to brave more than you think you can, and never will there be another like you.

You are your own rescue, answerable only to the infallible, omnipotent One.

Life is full of antecedents—preludes that steel us for the next skirmish or jubilation. Meanwhile, it can hamstring us again, like that night after my divorce, when I crashed and latched onto my wedding dress—uncertain if I could fly, walk, or crawl my way into daylight. If and when it does, I go back to these words:

> *"The ultimate measure of a man is not where he stands in moments of comfort and convenience, but where he stands at times of challenge and controversy."*
> - Dr. M. King, Jr.

Take your stance in faithfulness and rectitude, and leave the rest to Him. Under His blueprint, it'll all make sense.

> *"God will send the rain when He's ready. You need to prepare your field to receive it."*
> *- Facing the Giants*

David was a shepherd boy in the Valley of Eli in Israel. He didn't look like a monarch or a warrior, yet he was both. He herded his flock in the wilderness and protected them, using his sling—that was his strength—not the helmet, the coat of armor, or the sword Saul outfitted him—when the Philistines wanted to subjugate the Israelites.

David wasn't supposed to trounce the 6'9 infantry-clad giant with just a stick, a sling, and five stones, but he did. He wasn't supposed to prevail in warfare, but he did. He wasn't supposed to vanquish and decapitate Goliath, but he did. God had bestowed him a gift, and when outnumbered in both equipment and superiority, David used it and saved the encamped people of Israel from bloodshed.

David was exalted as a prophet. A ruler. A king.

In a showdown between you and your giants, know your mettle is impenetrable, your will, titanium. One more push, one more upsurge of valor, one more spate of prowess.

THIS. IS. YOUR. CHANCE. THIS. IS. YOUR. TIME.

David lives in me. David lives in you.

Undaunted. Indomitable. Victorious.

And should fear clobber your fortitude and faith, should all feel improbable and hopeless, and into each other should they bleed, remember your colors. Live by your creed.

MAHALO NUI LOA

You have no rival.
You have no equal.
Now and forever, God, You reign.
Yours is the kingdom.
Yours is the glory.
Yours is the name above all names.

What a powerful name it is.
What a powerful name it is.
The name of Jesus Christ, my King.

Lyrics: Ben Fielding & Brooke Ligertwood

My Mum, Josefina Delos Reyes Garcia

Forty-three years ago, in confusion, you thought your only choice was to make the mistake of keeping a child created out of sin or the mistake of aborting it, not knowing which would be bigger. I'm grateful you took a leap of faith. I'm grateful you're my mother. I'm grateful for your love for it could never be bested. You're my rock, my foundation, my gladiator, my fuel, my anchor—the extension of my being that my life would be unimaginable without. Wherever I am, you're with me. It's our time. It's *our* turn…

Salamat, Delos Reyes Ohana

Marian, Robert. Nikki, Nikko. Duke, DJ & Dale.

Maricel, Dhodee. Duane, Dwight. Chico, Daisy & Peanut.

Marineth, Gilbert. Gineth & Gianne.

Marlon & Anita.

For their kāko'o

Dr. Nikki Chun; B. Craft; D. Dias; Dr. Nick Einbender; Romelyn Fiesta; Ryan Garcia; Maan Herrera; Blyth Hirata. Candyce Kaaiai; Patricia Malagar; Lhen Manalo; Chipo Mathis; Spencer Mickelson; Marietta Morjan; Mia Proctor; Wayan Restiana; Joe Santiago; D. Saquilayan; Gail Takvar; Maria Teruya; Ismelda Vasquez; Yolanda Vineyard.

The Pencionados - thank you for your service.

Mishka Productions. My Fairy Godmother. My GW crew.

Shoutouts to these Rockstars:

Kyra & Todd Schaefer - I've waited my whole life to unlock this door to my magnum opus. You two are the key.

Dr. Claude McDowell - At the height of physical, mental, and emotional calamities (*self-created and otherwise*), way over my head—ready to jump on a grenade—I walked into your office, and life had been altogether different and better since that momentous day. You shielded me from whirling down with your sagacity, toughmindedness, brutal honesty, and even a pinch of pep talk. Peeling one disguise and one layer at a time. From marital thistles to corporate confluxes to my dingy past, you were the first stepping stone to my healing. Thank you for not handling me with kiddy gloves. You spurred me to stop reading other people's stories and to write my own. Five sentences later, you were the first to call me a "*writer.*" Here we are, Doc…

My Holy Trinity:

Jennifer Mitchell - We've been Bert & Ernie since fifth grade—that's thirty-one years of imperishable friendship! When it was sink or swim, Jenn had never left me astray. I've learned who'd lay on a shiv for me and who'd push me on it, and with Jenn, her loyalty had never been misplaced. After every heart-rending relationship, she reminded me to stay in faith and not let others glom my joy. My best friend and I can finish each other's sentences, telepathically share inside jokes, chortle uncontrollably without saying a word, and when we get goofy, they're no stopping us!

J. Nunez - We met in 1995 when I was only sixteen, and the terms of our indissoluble twenty-six-year-old friendship puzzle others as somewhat unorthodox. This much I'll say: I think the world of my late uncle, and there's only one man who's worthy of mentioning in the same breath as he: it's J.N. He's irreplaceable; life's unthinkable without him.

Those who'd asked me to choose between them and J.N. learned we're a deluxe package—I'm *not* giving him up. The first ninety days of divorce were hell, and I would *not* have made it without him. He held me together—piece by piece—sicced on me when I didn't even know, and helped me hold on, with open arms, until each tear became a rose. Keep tabs on me, Commander—my Pisces, my "*Hermosa*." Let's have twenty-six more years in a S'mores matrix, and "*where we go from there is a choice I leave to you.*"

Clay Perry – *Harold & Kumar* go way back to 1996! No red tape topic: puppy; pizza; politics. I'm my goofball self with him. This Einstein genius is my football coach, angel, I.T. tech, BFF. When life goes nuclear, he's never too far away to prop my spirits with boundless patience. He'd also foiled me from doing some dopy stuff in college. Without incertitude, my Clay-dough is there to affix my pieces anew when I bawl my insides out. This inviolable bond has no mask. What it does have is lots and lots of ridiculousness!

***

R.G. - When I was unbalanced, needing to blow off steam, she was there. When I was on a hospital bed, mopping and tachycardic, she was there. No proclamations of alliance, just deeds that helped me get out of the jam. Every time I thought she couldn't be a better friend, she outdid herself. Whatever R.G. does, she does it in uproarious style. She cautions me against renegades and steers me clear of the Benedict Arnolds—those who'd impugn your name to clear their own. Fiercely loyal, incredibly witty, reliable, real.

Kathy Hanson - If friendship had a name, it'd be Kathy. She's a trove of love and generosity. When others left me gutted, Kathy stood by me with staunch loyalty—and still does—high and low. She gets me out of my head when the squirrels up there are on meth without making me feel like I—and my tantrums—have outstayed our welcome. While many speak of solidarity, she shows it. That's support done right. From jocular to transcendental to discomfiting talks, Kathy's friendship and feedback are of the real kind.

April H. - We met in 2006 when we worked at Stanford hospital as travel nurses (*me in oncology, she, transplant*). We've gormlessly made some choices on and off the road, my sister in faith and me, and we lampoon each other and throw in a wisecrack here and there. But of the struggles and lessons that followed, we've become willful and wiser.

Neil Ifill - A dad, a husband, an artist, and a repository of wisdom. I knew his elevator went up the top floor during our M.S.M. program, and post-grad school, I realized my Barbados brother had a penthouse of life hacks. Only half of my brain and half of my labile heart functioned well in class, so I'm done. Neil continues to slog away at his Ph.D. This sharpshooter tells me when I'm overthinking life's peaks and troughs. Here's to you, Dr. Ifill!

P. Inocencio - I am as grateful welcoming you back into my life as you are grateful being welcomed. Twenty years seem fatuous, when you say nothing at all.

Mandie Lee - My equestrian friend and I met in 2007 at Johns Hopkins Hospital during our contracts. Traveling for us wasn't just a job; it was a lifestyle. We're both gypsies! During my divorce, I was inconsolable, but she never wrote me off. She piloted me into repose with undying patience, compassion, and wisdom, which helped me turn adversities into advantages. She's the most trustworthy person I know. We almost drowned side by side in Waimanalo, but still, she's my confidant and lifeguard—as pragmatic as one can be. The parallels of our past, present, and future go beyond these pages. She's all that is good in a person and a friend.

Martha Martinez - My former boss and forever friend. Months before the wedding, my then inebriated fiancé did something so asinine, I was ultra-livid—I kicked him out. We met at Cheesecake Factory where she said, *"Jodelene, when are you going to call this off? It's not too late, darling."* She was right, but I couldn't cancel. Invitations had gone out—all was in full swing, so I took him back. Seven years later, post-divorce, Martha was there for me. No, *"I told you so, Pendeja!"* No judgment—just love. She made me realize I have more to give and much to live for with a spectrum of possibilities. When I couldn't go any further, she stepped in and reminded me of the strength I had long kept submerged. A hero nurse and boss lady—but we know her fur babies run the show at home.

Shelbie McCain - A working mom and a military wife. (*Thank you for your service, Brandon!*) She also has a cat, a bird, chickens, and dogs. To say her plate is full won't cut it. It's sad to lose friends when you don't have many, but Shelbie had shown me that there's no time or distance for those who care about each other. My thoughtful friend makes time to connect and prop me with much cheeriness and support. This supermom is lovely inside and out.

Joe & Wendy Nadzady - I worked at Washington Hospital Center in 2006-2007, Joe was the house supervisor, and I had to up my game as in-charge or a nurse on the floor. No exemption or preferential treatment. When staff pushed my button and I'd quake from finding a patient post mortem, Joe was there with practical wisdom, an invocation, and/or a Bible verse to sedate the situation. At times, it's others who remind us of our real values. It's my honor to learn from his stewardship and leadership. In 2011, he read from the Book of Hebrews for my wedding. He & his beautiful wife Wendy were the most decorous and gracious guests. *Grazie, amico mio!*

Kenny North - Since 2008, it's all love between me and Kenny; alias *"my homie."* From the stages of D.C. to L.A, there's more to this telegenic actor than his comedy and art. He's a hard worker, sincere, and urbanely insightful in both diction and delivery. My go-to guy for *"man to man"* talks, pesky TV hitches (*I'm such a nuisance!*), and the History channel colloquies. He brings me Lo mein in the middle of the night, too. That's what's up!

D. Pae - My legal lexicon, a man of integrity, and a lawyer with a heart! Unlike turds who clamor for loyalty without returning the favor, he remains faithful to our friendship and his word, without snitching on me or betraying his own conscience. He helped me audit my perimeter of influence, and made me realize that within it, I'd settled for less, but never went for more. Don't let the culotte and cravat fool you! Though logical and linear in thinking, we can switch from *The Wall Street Journal* to TMZ very rapidly. And that $200 bet, future Justice…?

C. Pitman - When others ran, she stayed—no judgement. During my full-blown crisis (*at home and at work*), it was she—and only she—who showed up at my door with lattes, yoga mats, naan, eggplant tikka masala—whatever it took to pull me through. When all was said and done, when animus sent its flood, she was my life raft.

Virgil Santos - After the Great Breakup of 2008 with Ben, I stopped believing in romance and personal hygiene. Virg checked in on me, and right at the door, raised his hand like a scanner from my head down, and asked the now infamous question, *"What is thissssssssssssss—situation? Don't have a hairbrush?"* Acclimatized to my annual before-and-after breakup look—disheveled juxtaposed with disinfected—he babysat me and sterilized my pigsty apartment. I let myself go in marriage—indisputably—hoping if I were repulsive, fat, stinky & non-deodorized, my hubby wouldn't want me. I was in shabby clothes and a hundred times more unkempt during the divorce. I got my first professional haircut in ten years—all thanks to Virgil! He was (*and always is*) right: skipping on self-care was of no implication to anyone but myself. Friend, fashion police, world traveler, fitness buff, and #milliondollarnurse extraordinaire.

Sherry Shinmoto - Like a life coach, she'd brought new life to my world with her jolly spirit and exuberance. This mama got moxie! Through incremental progress, Sherry reintroduced me to my true loves: nature and travel. She made me realize being single wasn't a reason to not have fun—harmless fun. I reengaged in daily pleasures and felt alive again. Sherry helped me keep my feet on the ground when the pain's inescapable. On our 2019 Hilo trip, I said, *"I miss receiving texts from a guy saying how much he misses me."* She texted me, *"I miss you so much and you are next to me right this second."* We're like raucous teens laughing over mindless stuff.

SyRina Smith - Who has the emotional reservoir to put up with me when my head's in the clouds and the patience to lull my mind when I stress out more in imagination than in reality (*99.9% of the time*)? She does! What started as out as workplace chitchats, #savewater, #verbose, had evolved into a wonderful friendship. In the coming years after the tortuous toll (*and secrets*) of 2017, I was blessed to meet a friend with discretion, depth, and integrity. And if she also expands your awareness with self-diagnostic, constructive truth, what more could you ask for?

The love of my life

James Dean (*J.D.*) - Todo lo que siempre quise fue ser amado, y pensar, encontré a alguien (*con cuatro patas*) que quiera lo mismo. Me llenas de amor, esperanza, alegría, y risa, y nada me hace mas feliz que estar contigo y tus besos. Te amo como nunca antes amé.

And...

6/05 - I used to see the world without any shades of gray, and then I met you... And now, my heartbeat is the sound of your name because it wasn't my eyes you've opened— and I thank you for that.

I will

Never

Forget,

-JG

About The Author

JG Delos Reyes Garcia is a Philippine-born healthcare provider. She holds a B.S. from Johns Hopkins University, a B.A. from Notre Dame of Maryland University, and an M.S. from The Catholic University of America. She started her career at The Johns Hopkins Hospital and was a travel nurse for three years. Prior to leaving the mainland, she resided in Washington, D.C. while working for CareFirst BlueCross BlueShield. JG had written a piece for the book, *"Inspirations: 101 Uplifting Stories For Daily Happiness."* She's an animal aficionado, an amateur cupcake artist, and an avid fan of TED talks, Gibran, Poe, and Rumi. She'd seen three of the seven Worders of the World—so far—and all roads lead back to Bali. O'ahu is now her home, where she lives with James Dean—her mischievous Bichon Frisé.

jggarcia.com

www.ingramcontent.com/pod-product-compliance
Lightning Source LLC
LaVergne TN
LVHW051824080426
835512LV00018B/2716